T0358659

Challenges of Economic Growth, Inequality and Conflict in South Asia

Challenges of Economic Growth, Inequality and Conflict in South Asia

Proceedings of the 4th International Conference on South Asia
24 November 2008, Singapore

Edited by

Tan Tai Yong

Institute of South Asian Studies
National University of Singapore, Singapore

World Scientific

NEW JERSEY · LONDON · SINGAPORE · BEIJING · SHANGHAI · HONG KONG · TAIPEI · CHENNAI

Contents

Foreword

India's Challenge of Achieving Growth with Equity[1]

Tharman Shanmugaratnam

Minister for Finance, Singapore

All of us have a stake in India's ascendance. As the Prime Minister of India, Dr Manmohan Singh, said in an interview with the Hindustan Times on 21 November 2008, "The Indian experiment is not just India's ambition of the 21st Century, it is the global ambition". The world has a profound stake in both India and China's ascendance — in their ability to reform, grow and transform the lives of their populations.

Before I go on, let me say that I am no scholar of India. My comments are merely those of an interested observer from a country that wants to see India succeed and grow its presence in the world economy.

Three Major Positives

Let me start with the positives in India's recent experience, which give confidence in its future, before talking about the challenges that will have to be addressed.

The first major positive is that globalisation is working for India. The reforms that began in 1991 are basically working for India, regardless of which government has been in office. Everyone knows about the

---

[1] This is an edited transcript of the keynote address by Minister Tharman Shanmugaratnam, at the Fourth International Conference on South Asia, 24 November 2008.

remarkable growth of the information technology (IT) services industry. India has also seen, more generally, the creation of a confident middle-class that is engaged in one way or another in its interface with the global economy.

Globalisation is a large part of the explanation for the new growth trajectory that India is on. There will be occasional disruptions due to global crises or domestic events. However, it is fundamentally a different growth trajectory resulting from reforms to the Indian economy that have enhanced the benefits that can be reaped from globalisation, in goods and services and investments.

The two way flow of foreign direct investment (FDI) is an indication of this evolving process. What began with trade, especially in services and manufacturing, is now increasingly evident in the flow of FDI into and out of India. Last year, FDI into India was US$35 billion and FDI from India to rest of the world was US$19 billion. While these figures are still considered low, they are growing at an exponential rate. It reflects the mutual interest of both Indian and foreign firms in India's engagement in the global economy.

The second positive is the way domestic demand is spurring India's growing interface with the global economy. Even visiting India today, in the midst of a global crisis, what strikes one is the tremendous local appetite for things new. The growth of middle-class demand for better and more sophisticated goods and services is a powerful secular trend, the economic cycle notwithstanding. Healthcare illustrates this well. The growth in demand for quality healthcare in India over the next five years alone will be the largest seen in any country in the world over any five-year period in history. By 2011, it would need a doubling in the number of hospital beds compared to the current situation. Private enterprises are in the lead in this sector, with the setting up of hospitals and specialist enterprises which are no different in manpower quality from many of the best hospitals in more developed societies.

A third major positive is the shift in policy-making that has taken place over the years from one that is based on belief or economic ideology, to the one that is essentially driven by pragmatism. It is a fundamental shift in policy paradigm, towards seeking the best ways to utilise the energies of private businesses for the benefit of the country. That shift is intact regardless of who takes power in India. The businessmen see no fundamental differences in the economic approaches of the two major alliances — led by the Congress Party and the Bharatiya Janata Party. Both these major actors are fundamentally concerned with sustaining the momentum of economic growth and of eradicating poverty.

Underpinning these positives is a change in psychology, a certain confidence that India is now onto a very different dynamic trajectory. The 'Hindu rate of growth' is a vestige of the past. India knows it can now do what others in East Asia have done, that it will often do it in its own way with the same outcomes, and that it can sometimes do better. This confidence permeates society. It gives hope to new entrepreneurs who know that, despite the thicket of regulations they have to contend with, there will be a way forward. It gives hope even to the lower middle classes who now aspire to move up. This confidence is now a major asset for India.

No Inherent Trade-off between Growth and Equity

The deepest challenge for India and South Asia, as suggested by the theme of the conference, is that of continuing large inequality and the prevalence of poverty. As Indian Minister P. Chidambaram observed recently in the Field Marshal K.M. Cariappa Memorial Lecture, despite 18 years of reforms that began in 1991, the benefits of high growth have not trickled down to society. There have been improvements in agriculture and areas such as infant and maternal mortality, education and sanitation. But these improvements have been very slow, compared to India's overall rate of economic growth.

To a large extent, the same can be said about the rest of South Asia. If you look at the bottom 20 to 30 per cent of South Asia; and particularly the bottom 20 to 30 per cent of the rural population in the region, you see a sad picture of destitution and neglect.

There is, I believe, no inherent trade-off between achieving growth and equity. There will always be tensions between growth and equity in the short term. Fundamentally, however, the factors that constrain future growth in India are the same factors which constrain the eradication of poverty. Allow me to elaborate.

The broadest challenge that India faces in the coming decades is that of managing and encouraging the flow of people from low-productivity agricultural activities towards high-productivity urban economic activities, while, at the same time, raising the productivity of agriculture. It is the same big challenge which faced the Western societies and East Asia at corresponding times in their histories. We know that the remarkable economic advancement of Europe in modern times owed itself largely to the huge shift of people out of low-productivity rural livelihoods. In the United Kingdom, the Enclosure Acts of the 19th and 20th centuries, played a major role in industrialisation. Likewise the transformations seen in the post-war period in Japan, South Korea and Taiwan, and now taking place in China.

In growth accounting terms, by far, the most significant source of China's growth in the last two decades has been the shift of people from low-productivity rural activity, first to township and village enterprises and then to the whole range of urban activities with higher productivity on average than where they came from. The economists refer to this as enabling growth in 'total factor productivity'.

Raising rural productivity

It is in this transition from rural to higher-productivity urban activity that we see the most visible gap between India and China. In China, 47 per cent of the people now live in the cities, in India, about 22 per cent. Put another way, 78 per cent of the population in India lives in the rural sector, contributing to 60 per cent of the workforce, but only generating 20 per cent of the GDP. That illustrates the gulf in productivity levels of agriculture compared to the range of activities in the cities and towns.

Equally stark are comparisons of agricultural productivity itself. Yields in India have remained low and in the case of several crops, they are even declining. Take rice, for instance. India has roughly the same amount of arable land as China. In the best year, India produces 97 million tonnes of rice compared to about 130 million tonnes in China. That amounts to about a 30 per cent gap in agricultural productivity.

We know the causes — low public investment in irrigation, watershed management, inappropriate pesticides. There is generally low investment in India's rural sector. There are also endemic features of land ownership, particularly, land ceilings, preventing the growth of agriculture based on larger plots and larger scale. China has dealt with these issues in an interesting way. It retains the system of land ownership which assures farmers of their ownership rights. However, through rentals and other commercial means, it has been able to grow larger scale agriculture. In European and American economic history, large-scale agriculture came about through traditional capitalistic development.

Manufacturing is critical

A related angle to this problem for India has been the relatively limited absorption of labour into manufacturing. For labour to shift from low-productivity agriculture activity to high-productivity activity in the cities, we need growth in manufacturing. It employs the masses, and helps them develop skills. That is in fact the other big story in East Asia, how the engagement in manufacturing has led to a constant movement up in skills — of everyone, from the junior craftsman and the technician to the engineer and the research scientist. Engagement in a competitive global market has meant constant development of skills and productivity.

Manufacturing is critical for India's future. And we know from India's leading manufacturing companies that there is no lack of technological and organisational capability. Several of them are now a force in global markets. However, their spread in the Indian economy is limited, and the sector as a whole is not providing enough jobs. Further, the transition from heavy industry-oriented import-substituting industry towards labour-intensive, export-oriented manufacturing is a job only half done.

Here again, the problems are well told — excessive regulation, unions still caught in the mindset of a traditional protective economy and taxes that are extraordinarily high for a regular business corporation.

The services sector will not solve this problem. India's services make for international magazine stories on the country's ascendance. But as the World Bank calls it, Indian services are the camels in the infrastructural desert. They are also camels in a landscape where there are regulations at every turn — India's service exports have relied on the ingenuity of groups of individuals who were able to escape the bureaucratic maze. The basic point remains however that the number of people engaged in export-oriented services in India is extremely small. The IT services sector employs perhaps two to three per cent of graduates. It is not going to provide large-scale employment to educated people, let alone the less educated.

Raising agricultural productivity and moving more forcefully towards absorbing labour into factory employment, raising skills and competing internationally in manufacturing, must be the key strategies going forward, for both growth and the eradication of poverty.

Solutions that serve both growth and equity

What are the solutions, the ways to get there? I will highlight just two basic solutions, both well-known. The first is plugging major gaps in infrastructure. This is probably China's core competence and India's core incompetence — transport, power and water. With regard to water, in particular, states within India protect their own interests in ways that prevent efficient national solutions.

Investments in infrastructure will help solve problems of both growth and equity. The development of roads and electrification in rural areas will improve the lives of rural people. A proper infrastructure for manufacturing will enable the spread of jobs with better incomes and the prospect of moving up the skills ladder.

The second major solution lies in investments in social capital, in particular, education. Here too, there is a big gap between India and China. Even today, over half a century after independence and almost two decades after the economic reforms began, less than 60 per cent of Indian children in each age group complete primary school. Fewer still complete secondary school and a far smaller number go on to some form of post-secondary education.

In India, as it is across South Asia, there is a lack of safe drinking water, sanitation, basic health and education. And this too is not just an issue of social equity or of providing an opportunity for a decent life for the majority of the people. It is also an economic growth issue, because education, basic healthcare and sanitation are also the foundations for a fit and literate population that can spur growth, especially in manufacturing.

Leveraging on private sector capabilities

However, the Indian public sector, unlike say China's, is fiscally challenged. Both in terms of resources and methods, it is not well-equipped to sort out the challenges of infrastructure and social capital. However, investments in infrastructure, education and basic healthcare in India can benefit from partnership between the public and private sectors. One of the great strengths India has is in its highly competent private sector enterprises, who are now able to play a role in resolving infrastructural blockages as investments in rural social capital. The 11th Plan identifies the need to tap on private sector to set up technical colleges, for example.

There are also a whole range of social initiatives that are taking place not so much through government programmes, as through the energy of the Indian private sector and application of its best practices. For example, companies are using the IT services that they use in their corporate business to deliver basic healthcare — so that specialists in the cities or even abroad in places like the US, can link up with trained persons based in the villages to deliver heath services to rural folks. So there are strengths in India that can be leveraged on and India's way forward will be unique private-public partnership.

Appreciating India's Unique Historical Challenge

Any discussion of the challenges India faces must, however, recognise that India is attempting something that is unique in historical terms, which is to make the transition to industrialisation within an established democratic order. The United Kingdom made the transition, creating a large group of landless peasants and engaging them in what were initially low-wage industrial activities, before it introduced universal suffrage. China, where the other continental-scale transition to industrialisation and a liberal market order is taking place, is doing so without an electoral democracy.

What India is attempting is unique, and made more complex by a highly diverse society — far more diverse than Europe ever was, and certainly a far more ethnically differentiated society than China. One must admire what India has achieved in this context.

For some reason in India, since the early 1990s, the lower the caste, income and education of the person, the more likely it is that he will vote. In fact, the United Progressive Alliance government counts on the lower social economic groups as its most important constituency. It is an inversion of what happened in the West, where initially only the educated class was allowed to vote, and subsequently even with everyone having the right to vote, it is the better educated that tend to decide the outcome.

The key task for any political system is to be able to find the right trade-off between each group's interests and the shared interests of the whole, and the right trade-off between immediate gains and long-term prosperity. Observers in India have commented that the process of getting elected in India in the unique circumstances described above, has reduced the ability to make those choices and trade-offs in favour of the shared interests on the whole, and in favour of the longer-term investments and capabilities required for prosperity. Politics has been increasingly short-term, religion-based and caste-based in recent decades.

It does not appear that caste-based society itself is being reinforced. Some scholars, in fact, expect a continuing, albeit gradual, erosion of the caste system as people drift to the cities, especially to the factory floor, where everyone is equal on the production line regardless of social background or what caste they belong to. There is a gradual erosion of the caste-based society through migration.

However, in politics, caste-based affiliations have if anything been ascendant, and are much more present now than at the time of Independence. As Edward Luce, a journalist of the Financial Times, observed, "in India you do not cast your vote, but vote your caste," a pity phrase, but not a gross distortion of reality in certain Indian states.

Caste appears to be finding new expression in India because of competition within a meritocratic setting — in education and the job market. Competition for limited opportunities has led to those who fail to get on to the merit list feeling or claiming that they have been discriminated on the basis of caste. We have therefore seen a widening of the definition of caste in politics. A competitive job market and education system with limited opportunities is sustaining caste-based politics even as the underlying social forces are eroding the caste-based social order.

Conclusion

The world has a deep interest in India's continued growth. We know too that it cannot be sustained at the high levels seen in recent years without more concerted effort and progress in reducing poverty and wide inequalities in opportunity.

I believe we can be hopeful. If India addresses the basics — invests in the infrastructure needed to improve rural livelihoods and support the shift of people to towns and factory employment; and provides opportunities for the majority of its population of young people to stay through secondary school and obtain a post-secondary education education, we can be hopeful of its ability to sustain a growth trajectory of seven to eight per cent per year and achieve the trickle-down to society that has so far evaded it.

However, India's inability to make better progress in expanding opportunities and reducing poverty and, hence, in sustaining rapid economic growth, will ultimately depend on whether it can roll back the trend of its politics becoming more short-term, more religion-based and more caste-based.

Preface

It is well recognised that, while the advent of globalisation has ushered in a new era of economic growth and development in South Asia, the region remains mired in highly uneven and polarised growth patterns. The resultant increase in inequality generates its own problems and, in some cases, has contributed to social unrest, leading to tensions and conflicts. The global economic crisis may have caused further stress to this deep-seated economic malaise. With the onset of the crisis, most countries in the region have shown acute signs of vulnerability as they experience sharp decelerations in their export growth, following declining demands for their products from the West. This has led to a major slowdown in their industrial production, resulting in severe job losses which have significantly affected the vulnerable sections of their societies. Faced with such severe challenges, there is a growing need for South Asian policy makers to work out a clear roadmap for the future of the region — one that will enable them to sustain their economic growth momentum by addressing the diverse challenges they face.

This volume of conference papers extensively deals with these key issues and challenges facing South Asia today. The papers were written in conjunction with the Fourth International Conference on South Asia held in Singapore on 24 November 2008, focusing on the theme of 'Challenges of Economic Growth, Inequality and Conflict in South Asia'. These papers provide fresh insights into and analyses of the evolving economic, political and social landscapes of South Asia, focusing on both recent developments within the region and on the region's relations with the rest of Asia and the world at large.

The keynote address for the conference was delivered by Mr Tharman Shanmugaratnam, Singapore's Minister for Finance.

In his address, Shanmugaratnam focused on India's ascendancy as a regional and global economic power, largely due to its economic reforms. He underscored the importance of equitable economic growth for India, emphasising that there is no inherent trade-off between economic growth and equity. According to Shanmugaratnam, investments in infrastructure will contribute to the bridging of growth and equity.

In Chapter 1 of this volume, Arun Shourie discusses the complexity of the socio-economic and political issues shrouding India arising out of having a troubled neighbourhood. He highlights that the major factors originating from across the region that are likely to impact India in a significant way include the skewed patterns of development, evolving demography, adversarial view of India by a few countries and the deterioration of governance across the region in general, adding that India will have to pay much more attention and devote greater resources to its neighbours than it has done in the last 20 years. While acknowledging that India's immediate neighbours present many opportunities as well as challenges, he argues that in order to address these problems, India must, among other things, deepen its relations with countries beyond the South Asian region, extending them to Southeast Asia and Central Asia. Shourie maintains that India's most formidable challenge will be to tackle and compete with China in the long run, apart from dealing with its South Asian neighbours.

In Chapter 2, Shahid Javed Burki analyses the economic outlook for South Asia for the next two decades. While highlighting the growing consensus amongst economists about the shifting centre of gravity of the global economy towards the emerging world, he questions whether South Asia, as a region, can be included as part of this anticipated global shift. He argues that while it may be legitimate to count the countries of South Asia among the emerging markets, they still lag considerably behind the rest of the emerging world which is made up of the countries in East Asia, Latin America, North Africa, and South and Central Europe. He also emphasises that the heterogeneous growth patterns visible in different countries in South Asia are primarily due to their inherent structural problems, and corrective measures to address these structural problems are prerequisites for the region to move to higher growth trajectories. Burki adds that what happens to the economies of South Asia in future will depend more on domestic public policies that the countries adopt.

Saman Kelegama takes a closer look at the growing global trade and investment linkages in the South Asian region and some of the broad contours surrounding this pattern of growth in Chapter 3. He highlights the areas that have contributed to the overall rise of South Asia and discusses the possible ways to sustain this process over the long run. The central message he tries to convey from his analysis is that there is an urgent need for regional economic integration within South Asia and that a number of opportunities which can provide a 'win–win' outcome for all the countries at the individual level remain unexploited.

In Chapter 4, Praful C. Patel deals with the crucial issue of poverty that South Asia has been grappling with for decades. He provides an in-depth analysis of the journey that the South Asian countries have traversed in dealing with poverty since the time of their independence. He highlights the critical priorities that will have to be adopted to reduce the levels of poverty in the region, namely, accelerated and sustained high economic growth rates; faster and greater progress in human development; and inclusive development. Patel adds that the key obstacles to ending poverty — inequality, inadequate infrastructure, lagging human development and weak governance — are man-made and, hence, can be dismantled the same way they were erected.

Salehuddin Ahmed presents a succinct analysis of the problem of inflation in South Asia in Chapter 5. He examines the present trends of inflation and growth in the South Asian countries and suggests policy options to manage inflation at reasonable levels. While acknowledging that moderating inflation and raising economic growth at the same time in South Asia will require painful trade-offs, he stresses the need for coordinated monetary and fiscal measures to contain inflation and achieve higher growth for which it will also be desirable to firmly anchor inflation expectations pre-emptively and decisively.

In Chapter 6, Peter Reeves discusses the role of the Indian diaspora and its economic activities. He focuses on the way Indian entrepreneurs have used 'acquisition and merger' activities to establish their industrial presence in this region in the context of international policy changes. He also discusses India's reassessment of the role of diasporic or non-resident Indian entrepreneurs after the economic 'reforms' of the early 1990s.

In Chapter 7, Bibek Debroy highlights the influence of India's soft power and its cultural influence on the world. While showing that the post-1991 economic reforms and the country's growing economic clout de-linked Indian soft power from its historical religious overtones, he argues that, consequent to India's liberalisation programme, there has been a visible increase in India's soft power influence. Debroy states that 'a country's soft power rests upon the attractiveness of its culture, the appeal of its domestic political and social values, and the style and substance of its foreign policies', and adds that India has to deal with its problem of an overly-bureaucratised government for its soft power influence to be possibly more effective in future.

Stephen Jones and Ramlatu Attah review the key challenges for developing infrastructure policies in South Asia in the final chapter. They set out a characterisation of the main features of infrastructure that make its provision by either the private or public sector problematic as well as the routes by which infrastructure impacts economic growth, and the main lessons from recent international experience. They note that, according to available evidence, South Asia trails many other parts of the developing world in important aspects of infrastructure access (notably in relation to the power sector), while plausible estimates suggest that investment in infrastructure in the region needs to increase by approximately threefold to sustain recent economic growth rates. Jones and Attah add that the international financial crisis will make the task of raising international capital for infrastructure projects more difficult, but it may create additional incentives for policy and financial sector reforms to encourage more domestic financing.

The papers presented at the Institute of South Asian Studies' Fourth International Conference on South Asia address some of the most pressing economic and developmental issues facing South Asia.

I am confident that this volume of papers will strengthen the existing body of work available on a theme that has not only aroused the interests of many, but has also tremendous economic and strategic significance.

Professor Tan Tai Yong
Director
Institute of South Asian Studies

About 'The International Conference on South Asia'

The International Conference on South Asia brings together academic specialists as well as leaders in the world of affairs to provide fresh insights into and analyses of the evolving economic, political and social landscapes of South Asia. It focuses on both recent developments within the region and also on the region's relations with the rest of Asia and the world at large.

Launched in 2005, the conference is the flagship event of the Institute of South Asian Studies. It was prompted by the need to understand South Asia from a variety of perspectives and to examine avenues for greater cooperation and collaboration throughout Asia and especially among South Asian neighbours.

The present volume is the fourth in a series devoted to publishing the proceedings of this annual event. Given the growing political and economic weight of South Asia in the world, the analyses and deliberations contained in this series deserve to be aired across a wide audience within and outside South Asia.

About the Contributors

Tharman Shanmugaratnam is the Minister for Finance in Singapore. He has served in various positions in the economic and education ministries since his entry into politics in 2001, including five years as Minister for Education between August 2003 and March 2008. He was appointed Minister for Finance in December 2007.

Tharman spent much of his earlier professional life at the Monetary Authority of Singapore, Singapore's central bank and integrated financial regulator, where he was chief executive before he entered politics in October 2001.

He is currently also Deputy Chairman of the National Research Foundation and serves on the boards of the Government of Singapore Investment Corporation and the MAS. He is in addition Chairman of the Ong Teng Cheong Institute of Labour Studies, and Chairman of the Council of Advisors of the Singapore Industrial and Services Employees Union.

Tharman is Chairman of the Board of Trustees of the Singapore Indian Development Association, which seeks to uplift educational aspirations and strengthen resilience in the local Indian community.

Tharman obtained undergraduate and masters degrees in Economics from the London School of Economics and Cambridge University. He later obtained a masters degree in Public Administration at Harvard University, where he received the Lucius N Littauer Fellow award.

He is married to Jane Yumiko Ittogi, a lawyer. They have four children, three boys and a girl, all of school-going age.

Salehuddin Ahmed joined as the Governor of the Bangladesh Bank (Central Bank of Bangladesh) on 2 May, 2005. Ahmed was the Managing Director of Palli Karma-Sahayak Foundation, the apex funding agency of micro credit operations in Bangladesh. He obtained his PhD in Economics from McMaster University, Canada in 1978.

He started his career as a teacher in Economics at Dhaka University and then joined the civil service of the Government in the erstwhile Civil Service of Pakistan cadre. He served in various capacities in the field of administration in the Government of Bangladesh. He worked at the centre on Integrated Rural Development for Asia and the Pacific, a regional inter-governmental organisation with its headquarter in Dhaka. He was the Director General of Bangladesh Academy for Rural Development, Comilla and also Director General of the Non-government Organisation Affairs Bureau of the Office of the Prime Minister. He has authored more than 60 books, reports and journal articles which have been published at home and abroad. He is on the advisory bodies of several government and non-government agencies in Bangladesh. He has travelled extensively in many countries of the world.

Shahid Javed Burki was educated at Oxford University as a Rhodes Scholar and at Harvard University as a Mason Fellow, and spent most of his professional life at the World Bank where he held a number of senior positions, including Director of China and Mongolia Department (1987–1994) and Vice-President Latin America and the Caribbean (1994–1999). He took leave of absence from the Bank to take up the position of Pakistan's Finance Minister (1996–1997). He is currently Chairman, The Institute of Public Policy, a Lahore, Pakistan think tank. He resides in Washington.

Bibek Debroy was educated in Presidency College, University of Calcutta, Kolkata (BA Economics, 1973), Delhi School of Economics, University of Delhi (MA Economics, 1976) and Trinity College, University of Cambridge (MSc Economics, 1981).

He has held the following positions: Research Associate, Presidency College, Kolkata (1979–1983); Associate Professor, Gokhale Institute of Politics and Economics, University of Poona, Pune (1983–87); and Professor, Indian Institute of Foreign Trade, Delhi (1987–1993). In 1993, he quit a teaching career to head a project on law reforms in India, started by the Indian Ministry of Finance and the United Nations Development Program. This project was named "LARGE" and lasted from 1993 to 1998. In between, from 1994 to 1995, he was also a Consultant with the Department of Economic Affairs, Ministry of Finance. In 1995, he was the Chief Consulting Economist with the National Council of Applied Economic Research in New Delhi. From 1993 to 1998, he was a Visiting Professor at the National Law School University of India in Bangalore. From 1997 to 2004, he was the Director of the Rajiv Gandhi Institute for Contemporary Studies, Rajiv Gandhi Foundation. From 2005 to 2006, he was the Secretary General of the Punjab, Haryana and Delhi Chamber of Commerce and Industry in New Delhi. From January 2007, he has been Professor at the International Management Institute, New Delhi, and from April 2007, Research Professor at Centre for Policy Research in New Delhi.

Bibek is a member of the Mont Pelerin Society and of the National Manufacturing Competitiveness Council. He has been a member of several government-appointed task forces, committees and commissions. He is also on the board of some Indian companies and on the governing boards of research institutes such as the National Institute of Public Finance and Policy. In 2006 and 2007, he was the rapporteur for one of the working groups in the United Nations Commission on Legal Empowerment for the Power. He has also undertaken consultancy work for several organisations. With Laveesh Bhandari as a co-author, he has published several inter-state comparisons and the annual ranking he worked on for "*India Today*" is often quoted.

From 1995, Bibek has been a regular columnist and consulting/contributing editor with various newspapers/magazines such as Business Standard, Financial Express and Telegraph. At present, he is a contributing editor with the Indian Express group (*Indian Express* and *Financial Express*).

Stephen Jones is an economic consultant with Oxford Policy Management and has a wide range of experience of working on development issues in Africa, Asia (including Bangladesh, India and Pakistan) and other parts of the world.

He was commissioned by the Asian Development Bank (ADB) to prepare a study of the linkages between infrastructure and poverty as part of the joint ADB/World Bank/JBIC study on "Connecting East Asia" and subsequently prepared a background paper for the

United Kingdom government's "Asia 2015" Conference in London in 2006.

Ramlatu Attah joined Oxford Policy Management (OPM), United Kingdom, in September 2008 as an Assistant Consultant, providing research support to the Social Policy Programme. At OPM, Ramlatu's work has focused mainly on countries in South Asia, East Asia and Sub-Saharan Africa. She has experience working on growth and infra-structure issues, natural resource management and HIV/AIDS.

She holds an MSc in Development Economics from the Institute for Development Policy and Management, University of Manchester. Prior to joining OPM, she worked as an intern at the Department for International Development — Latin America Department, where she was part of the Regional Assistance Plan evaluation team.

Saman Kelegama is the Executive Director of the Institute of Policy Studies of Sri Lanka. He is a Fellow of the National Academy of Sciences of Sri Lanka and was the President of the Sri Lanka Economic Association (SLEA) during 1999–2003.

He has published extensively on Sri Lankan and regional economic issues in both local and international journals. His latest books are *South Asia in the WTO* (Sage: 2007), *Development under Stress: Sri Lankan Economy in Transition* (Sage: 2006), *Contemporary Economic Issues: Sri Lanka in the Global Context* (SLEA: 2006), *Economic Policy in Sri Lanka: Issues and Debates* (Sage: 2004), and *Ready-Made Garment Industry in Sri Lanka: Facing the Global Challenge* (IPS: 2004). He is the co-editor of the *South Asia Economic Journal* (Sage Publication).

He serves and has served on a number of government and private sec-tor Boards as an independent member. He is a member of the National Economic Council under the President of Sri Lanka. He received his Doctorate (D.Phil.) in Economics from University of Oxford, U.K.

Praful Patel, a Ugandan national, was one of the senior corporate leaders of the World Bank. He served as the Vice-President of South Asia from 1 July 2003 to 30 June 2008. During that period, the World Bank programme in the South Asia Region was substantially scaled up with a sharp focus on poverty reduction and high growth rates in all of the region's countries. The World Bank's programme under his oversight comprised an average of US$4.5 billion of new project funding annually, and a portfolio of over 170 projects worth US$20 billion under implementation as of 2008. Praful was responsible for a staff of 700 in Washington and five country offices in South Asia with a budget of over US$140 million.

Praful joined the World Bank in 1974 through the Young Professional Program after completing his higher education at the University of Nairobi in Kenya, Royal Academy of Fine Arts in Denmark and later the Massachusetts Institute of Technology in the United States. In his long career in the Bank, Praful has provided strategic leadership in managerial and corporate positions in various parts of the Bank taking forward the institution's mission of poverty alleviation in regions as varied as Africa, East Asia, Latin America, Northern Africa and the Middle East.

In the process, Praful has covered different programmes including poverty reduction, regional integration, urban, infrastructure, private sector, financial sector and macro-economic management. Praful's management skills and experience have also been called upon to support the Bank's institutional agenda. He has held senior management positions in country programme departments, sector departments as well as regional management.

He has effectively led the World Bank Group's Appeals Committee, supported the development of country teams, and played a primary role representing the Bank in developing and implementing the Africa Capacity Building Program. He has also taken on senior management oversight of complex Bank-supported initiatives in countries confronting major macro-economic shocks, post-conflict countries, and countries involving international cross-boundary undertakings, and piloted in Southern Africa the Bank's increasing shift to country dialogue based on knowledge management and support of local capacity. After a career spanning 35 years at the World Bank, Praful retired in August 2008 and continues to work on development in South Asia and Africa.

Peter Reeves, Emeritus Professor of South Asian History at Curtin University (Perth, Western Australia), was Visiting Professor and Head of the South Asian Studies Programme at the National University of

Singapore from June 1999 to December 2006. A Fellow of the Academy of Humanities in Australia, he has also taught at the universities of Sussex, Western Australia and Michigan. His research interests are in the following areas: the political and agrarian history of northern India; the maritime history of the Indian Ocean since 1800; the history of fisheries in colonial and postcolonial South Asia; the history of Singapore's inshore and culture fisheries; and the history of the Indian diaspora. He was Executive Editor of *The Encyclopaedia of the Indian Diaspora* (Singapore: Editions Didier Millet, October 2006) and, with Dr Rajesh Rai he co-edited, *The South Asian Diaspora. Transnational Networks and Changing Identities* (London: Routledge, 2008).

Arun Shourie is among India's best known commentators on current and political affairs. Born in Jalandhar, Punjab (1941), he studied at St. Stephen's College in Delhi and then obtained his doctorate in Economics from Syracuse University, United States.

Among other portfolios, he held the office of the Minister of Disinvestment, Communications and Information Technology in Mr Atal Bihari Vajpayee's cabinet. He was acclaimed as a "Star of Asia" by Business Week in 2002, and as "The Business Leader of the Year" by The Economic Times jury for his pioneering and dogged work on privatisation. In a poll of Indian Chief Executive Officers, he was acclaimed as "The Most-outstanding Minister" of Mr Vajpayee's government in early 2004.

He is the recipient of numerous national and international awards, including the Magsaysay Award, and one of India's highest civilian awards, the Padma Bhushan.

He has been an economist with the World Bank, and Editor of the Indian Express. He is widely regarded as the initiator of Investigative Journalism in India. The International Press Institute, Vienna, acclaimed him as one of 50 "World Press Freedom Heroes" whose work has sustained freedom of the press in the last half-century.

He has written 21 books on a variety of topics, ranging from constitutional law, modern Indian history, religious fundamentalism, governance in India, to national security.

His latest book, *The Parliamentary System: What We Have Made of It, What We Can Make of It*, was released in May 2007.

About the Editor

Tan Tai Yong, a Professor of History, was appointed Director of the Institute of South Asia Studies on June 1, 2008. He is concurrently Dean of the Faculty of Arts and Social Sciences at the National University of Singapore.

He has written extensively on South Asian history as well as on Southeast Asia and Singapore. His recent books include Creating *'Greater Malaysia'*: *Decolonisation and the Politics of Merger* (2008); *Partition and Post-Colonial South Asia*: *A Reader* (co-edited, 2007); *The Garrison State* (2005), *The Aftermath of Partition in South Asia* (co-authored, 2000) and *The Transformation of Southeast Asia: International Perspectives on De-colonisation* (co-edited, 2003).

About the Institute
of South Asian Studies

The Institute of South Asian Studies was established in July 2004 as an autonomous research institute within the National University of Singapore. Its establishment reflects the increasing economic and political importance of South Asia, and the strong historical links between South Asia and Southeast Asia.

ISAS is dedicated to the study of contemporary South Asia. It generates knowledge and insights about South Asia, and disseminates them in a manner that is useful to policy-makers, the business community, academia and civil society.

ISAS is actively engaged in developing research programmes and generating publications on South Asian economics, politics and international relations. It also organises regular conferences, seminars, lectures, roundtable sessions and workshops to promote general, academic and public awareness of South Asia. At the same time, it interacts with government agencies, the University, civil society and the business community; and establishes linkages with international bodies such as centres of South Asia research worldwide.

List of Tables and Figures

Tables

Chapter 2

Chapter 3

Chapter 5

Chapter 8

Figures

Chapter 3

Chapter 4

Chapter 5

Chapter 8

Box

Chapter 3

Chapter 1

Bal Howa Bandhan Kate...
India and Its Neighbours[1]

Arun Shourie

India's neighbourhood is in flux. It is troubled. The flux will swirl at an even faster pace in the coming years. And the troubles within the countries around India, as well as the trouble they are liable to cause India too seem set to intensify.

It is not just that several of its neighbours — China, Pakistan, Bangladesh — have definite agendas *vis á vis* India, several of the steps that they are liable to take for meeting their own circumstances are certain to have major consequences for India. To cite an instance to which we shall return, Chinese authorities state that as many as 600 cities and towns in China are today short of water, that the water situation in 200 of them is "critical". To meet this shortage, China has begun drawing up plans, and has begun preliminary engineering work to divert Tibet's waters to the north. This is bound to have grave consequences for north and east India, as it will for Bangladesh which is equally dependent on the Brahmaputra, and the Southeast Asian countries that depend on the Mekong.

Accordingly, one of the features that stands out as we look 20 years ahead is that India will have to pay much more attention to, and devote much greater resources to its neighbours than it has been doing in the last 20 years.

---

[1] An earlier version of this paper was prepared for the study, *India 2039*, that is being done by The Centennial Group under the auspices of the Asian Development Bank. The phrase 'Bal Howa Bandhan Kate' literally means 'If there is strength; it will remove constraints..."

Five General Factors

Before we consider specific developments in its neighbours that will affect India and how it should prepare to respond to them, we should note five general factors originating in, and concerned with its neighbours that are certain to impact India in ways that are vital to its prospects.

Foremost among these is the impact that the pattern of development in its neighbours, as well as in India itself is liable to have on the ecology of and around India. For instance:

- Denudation of eastern Tibet and intensified exploitation of mineral and other resources within Tibet by China will contribute to accelerating the pace at which Himalayan glaciers are already melting. As all the major rivers of north India, except the Ganges, originate in the Tibetan plateau, such acceleration will affect every aspect of life in the subcontinent.
- India, in particular, eastern India, is already suffering severely from the consequences of illegal migration from Bangladesh, about 20 million Bangladeshis are estimated to have crossed into India. They have exacerbated social, ethnic and political tensions across eastern India. If, to the factors that have been hitherto causing and facilitating this influx, is added the effect of climate change — the rise of the sea-level and the consequential submergence of large swaths of Bangladesh, in particular, of the densely populated coastal areas — the movement of Bangladeshis into India will assume the proportions of a disaster.
- Overexploitation of the Indus in its upper reaches has begun to cause extensive salination of the soil in Sindh, just as its reduced flow is beginning to cause ingress of the sea. Slower development in Pakistan as well as uncertainties that bedevil the country have already begun to cause migrants to cross over the Indian border — the 2000 Census revealed that villages had sprung up on the Indian side, in Rajasthan, that did not exist even ten years earlier. If on top of these factors, ecological deterioration of this kind continues, India will be faced with an influx from the west to

compound the problems that arise today from influx of illegal migrants from Bangladesh.

The second feature that will have major consequences is the evolving demography of the region:

- Unemployment rates are already high in Pakistan, Nepal and Bangladesh. At current rates of growth, the numbers of unemployed are certain to increase. On top of these realities of the present, the population in these states is continuing to grow at a rapid rate: Pakistan, with a population that already exceeds that of Russia, is expected to add another 70 million between 2000 and 2020 — almost half its total population in 2000; Nepal is expected to add 46 per cent to its 2000 population of 24 million; Bangladesh is expected to add 53 million, over 40 per cent of its 2000 population of 130 million.

- In case growth in these neighbouring countries continues to be inadequate and of a nature that does not create a sufficient number of jobs, ever-larger numbers will keep moving into India in search of a livelihood.

- It is not just that the pressure on resources and the consequential tensions within India will intensify; such large additions to the population of neighbours will have other deep consequences for the region as a whole. To cite just one instance, those professing religions native to South Asia constituted about 74.4 per cent of the population at the turn of the 20th century. By now, the proportion has fallen to about 68 per cent. Furthermore, as not only are the rates of growth of the population of different religious communities qualitatively different, as the additional numbers are concentrated in specific regions, the effects on inter-communal harmony are much greater than the overall numbers would suggest. Again, to take just one instance that has been a matter of much concern within India, the differential rates of population growth among religious communities compounded by the influx from Bangladesh have so altered the demographic balance in the border districts of eastern India that the highest authorities, such as T.V. Rajeswar, the former head of the Intelligence Bureau and Governor of West Bengal and currently the Governor of Uttar Pradesh; and General S.K. Sinha, former Deputy Chief of Army Staff and Governor of Assam and Jammu and Kashmir, have warned of the prospect of a third Islamic Republic being carved out of India in the coming decades.

Third, at least three countries of the region have a definite and adversarial view of India. These are China, Pakistan and Bangladesh. We shall deal briefly with each of these later on, but two general features should be noted at the outset. First, they are by now well knit; in particular in regard to the steps they shall take *vis á vis* India. Second, while the principal cause of instability, violence, deaths within India is the continuing and pervasive power of the military-*mullah* complex within Pakistan, it is evident that the principal props of Pakistan are not going to move to restrain or deflect it in the foreseeable future. Arming, equipping and standing by Pakistan are an important instrument of Chinese policy towards this region. Similarly, Saudi Arabia will neither dilute its support for this important Sunni state nor use its influence to alter Pakistan's policies towards India. The United States has today the greatest influence as far as the governmental apparatus of Pakistan is concerned. However, as the double standards it has adopted in regard to the proliferation activities of Pakistani scientists like A.Q. Khan and the terrorist depredations that its agencies have continued to inflict show, at the time this chapter is being written, the United States feels itself to be so dependent on Pakistan that it will not use the influence it has to actually deflect Pakistan from its hostile actions against India.

Fourth, with the exception of Bhutan, each of India's smaller neighbours harbours apprehensions that are common to small neighbours of large states. The population of each of them — and of course, of Bangladesh and Pakistan too — has deep cultural and religious affinities with the population across the country's border with India. All of them were part of the same British sphere of influence, and, in the case of Myanmar, Sri Lanka, Bangladesh, Pakistan and India, of the same British Empire in South Asia. Moreover, a country like Nepal is economically dependent on India. Precisely because their populations are culturally and religiously akin to their neighbours in India, precisely because they have shared a common history till so recently, these countries are all the more anxious to affirm that they are different. Precisely because a country like Nepal is economically dependent on India, cooperating in any project with India is a major and, hitherto, insuperable political issue within the country. Furthermore, to safeguard itself, India has to aim to be strong enough to stand up to China — but the more it does so, the more apprehensive its smaller neighbours become of India. Two consequences follow. First, these neighbours will seek every opportunity to play China and India off against each other: it is no accident that all the countries of the region, save Bhutan, moved to admit China into the South Asian Association for Regional Cooperation (SAARC) with an Observer status. Hence, the second consequence: India will have to devote enormous effort and very substantial resources to assuage the anxieties of its smaller neighbours.

The fifth general development in the neighbours that will impact India is the deterioration of governance across the region. In several swaths of each of its neighbours, as in vast stretches of India itself, governance has virtually evaporated. The writ of the state no longer runs in them — the writ of the local terrorist organization, of the smugglers' network, of the local don is what determines what will happen: whether this be who shall get the contract for executing a government "development project" or it be who shall prevail in a land dispute. Apart from the other consequences that this inflicts, the resulting vacuum clears space and opportunity for non-state forces. Several terrorist groups operating in India have had state sponsorship — for instance, that of Pakistan's army and intelligence agencies. But, in addition, several groups are becoming increasingly self-sufficient: they are able to raise resources through extortion — for instance, from contractors carrying out projects financed by the respective governments. These groups — secessionist groups like the United Liberation Front of Assam (ULFA) in the northeast; the Naxalites from the border with Nepal to the edge of Karnataka; the Islamic terrorist groups — have linkages across countries of the region — through arms dealers, through *hawala* operators, through smugglers' networks. As a result, even apart from the consequences that befall it because of the singular aim of a country like Pakistan, India will have to contend with these ominous tumours that now extend across the region.

Twelve General Prescriptions

Each of these general features dictates imperatives for India, imperatives that will become evident as we review prospects and options *vis á vis* individual neighbours. Twelve general prescriptions, however, can be noted even at this stage:

- In spite of the difficulties that surround it, in a sense, as one way to deal with them, India must grow rapidly, acquiring what the Chinese correctly characterise "Comprehensive National Strength". That growth may stimulate others who are today caught up in creating trouble for themselves and others to redirect their energies. It will give India the sinews to meet the challenges that it faces, including those from a neighbour like China. It will give India the opportunity to try and co-opt some of its neighbours in growth so that their own prosperity gets intertwined with India's continuing growth.
- India will have to reverse the current pattern of its policies, a pattern marred by three features:
  - o Half-hearted and hesitant — initiatives are begun, at the minuscule scale of pilot projects, and they remain at that scale; to make a dent, the policies will have to be robust and India's initiatives and interventions will have to be of a qualitatively larger scale;
  - o Piecemeal — contrast the way each ministry and state in India deals with multinationals with the coordination between all agencies and levels of government that firms experience when they invest in China; and
  - o Here today and soon forgotten: to meet the challenges that it faces in its neighbourhood as well as to seize the opportunities that lie in the future, policies will have to be pursued for decades at a stretch.

- India's policies will have to be omni-directional: challenges will come from, opportunities will lie, in all quarters — it will have to deal with and harness all of them.
- India must differentiate its neighbours into four groups. China as a class in itself; Pakistan and Bangladesh; the smaller neighbours adjacent to India; and countries in its extended security horizon — countries in the Middle East and Central Asia in one direction and those in Southeast and East Asia in the other. As we shall see, India will have to devise differing approaches to each group.
- In particular, in regard to the small countries adjacent to it, India must be as accommodating and as generous as any country can possibly be, and then some more — offering them assistance on a scale and on terms that will allay their apprehensions. As cooperating in projects originating from, in projects some part of the benefits from which will go to India meets with considerable resistance within each of these countries, India should invite organisations like the Asian Development Bank (ADB) to devise and champion projects which India and its smaller neighbours can undertake together.
- Where regional issues make interventions unavoidable — whether these concern Tamils in Sri Lanka or the Maoists in Nepal — India will have to act much more energetically. And it must do so in the certain knowledge that its initiatives in such matters will meet initially with stiff resistance — witness what Pakistan has been doing to thwart even its development work in Afghanistan; witness how it has prohibited even humanitarian supplies from India being sent across to Afghanistan *via* the land route.
- Develop the capacities to mete out, and by its record establish that it is a country that *will* mete out severe retribution on the country and group that breaches its security and sovereignty.
- Devote a great deal of effort to partner with countries in its extended security horizon: developing close partnerships with countries such as Afghanistan and the Central Asian republics will be one way to deal with Pakistan, and balance China; partnering with Myanmar in developing its northern ports and building the road from Sittwe to Mizoram will be one way to convince Bangladesh that routes through it are not the only ways to India's

northeast, partnering with Myanmar in exploiting its natural gas will be one way to make Bangladesh see that its dog-in-the-manger policies in regard to its own gas reserves end up hurting Bangladesh alone.

- Join every effort to strengthen international regimes on climate change, as well as on the rights of riparian States.
- Develop alliance systems: to deal with Islamic terrorism, and with China.
- Engage intensely with the international community in regard to each of its neighbours: How is Pakistan to be kept from continuing as the pivot of terrorism and disruption? What measures will keep Islamic fundamentalism from commandeering Bangladesh? What can all do together to shore up states in the region that have failed, that are failing, those that are flailing?
- Indeed, to keep in the coming 20 years from aggravating problems the way they have been aggravated during the last twenty, education of an even more elementary degree is required — both for India and for the West. Have they not shut their eyes to what those who control Pakistan have been doing, and instead relied on "hope as policy"? Have they not been giving in to blackmail? Have they not ever so often rewarded criminality? Is the "core issue" Kashmir? Is it even terrorism? Or is it the nature of the state and society of Pakistan? Confusion, wishful thinking, and downright refusal to face facts on these matters have cost India dearly in the last two decades. To face the next two, it must clarify its mind on them, and then engage intensely with the world on each of them.
- Use its advantages, its "soft power" much more, and much more creatively: the lure that audiences in the Middle East and Central Asia have for its films; the goodwill it would earn if only it were to set out to so expand and improve its medical facilities that it would become the surgeon of choice for all neighbours; if only it were to so improve and expand its facilities for higher and technical education that, instead of its youth going abroad for study, youth from all these countries would come to India as the educator of choice.

China: In the Long Run, the Most Formidable Challenge

As India plans for the next 20 years, it is vital for India to bear in mind several features about China:

- China's civilisational thrust has been the acquisition of power, the exercise of power, the manipulation of the symbols of power.
- Throughout, China has been determined to control its periphery. Because technology now enables distant countries — say, the United States — to constitute a threat to it, China strives to develop capacities to influence and control countries at that distance also. After the conquest of Tibet by China, India, in any case, lies literally on the periphery of China.
- China is an intensely nationalist country: Mao is revered today not so much as a Communist leader as much as a leader who fought resolutely against the Japanese and who then made China stand up to the world; the intense nationalist pride that the Chinese felt at the Olympics points to the same trait. Both strength, and sudden difficulties — as the failure of the Great Leap Forward in 1958 and the famine of 1960/61 — can trigger the Chinese rulers to seek to divert the people through a nationalist lunge at others.
- China has completely overhauled its strategic doctrine. It has moved a long way from "peoples war" which aimed at luring the aggressor deep into China and then overwhelming him; to "modern warfare under high-technology conditions" which aimed to equip China to resist the aggressor at its borders; to "force projection" and "total war". The earlier doctrines were of concern only to those who may have intended to move forces against China. The current doctrine impinges directly on the future prospects of a country like India. And China is rapidly acquiring capacities for force projection as well as "total war".
- China has a definite view about India — that it is a potential nuisance, and that it is one of the claws of the crab, the crab being the United States which seeks to contain China. China, therefore, aims to contain India and keep it busy within South Asia.

- In doing so, it has an enthusiastic instrument in Pakistan and willing partners among several elements in Bangladesh.
- In pursuit of this view of India, China has moved to ring India. It has, in fact, gone far towards doing so: Pakistan as an ally; a fully militarised Tibet, a Tibet that is a major base for Chinese land, missile, nuclear forces; a military pact with Bangladesh; Myanmar as a dependency. It has acquired Coco Islands on an indefinite lease from Myanmar — the islands are just 30 nautical miles from Andaman and Nicobar; it is developing Chittagong in Bangladesh, Hambantota in Sri Lanka and Gwadar and Ormara in Pakistan as naval bases, and as places at which it will have at the least port and bunker facilities.
- Since the victory of Maoists in Nepal, reports have become increasingly incessant of China planning to extend the Lhasa railway to Kathmandu, and its extensive road network in Tibet to several points in Nepal. Looking 20 years down the line, it would be altogether unrealistic for India to assume that tiny Bhutan will be able to stave off China's overtures and influence. In a word, the extension of China's presence and influence on to the southern slopes of the Himalayas will almost certainly come to prevail in the period covered by this study. And that will mark another milestone for India.
- Through moves such as the Kunming Initiative, China has also indicated its intention to endeavour to co-opt the northeastern states of India into its economic co-prosperity sphere.

These strategic measures are but a part of the scenario that India will have to confront *vis à vis* China in the coming twenty years. Several other aspects of China's rise, and several other plans that it has already set in motion will come to impinge heavily on India's prospects in the coming decades. There is place here to mention just one of them.

As we noted in passing above, according to Chinese authorities, 600 cities and towns of China face water shortage; in 200 of them, the scarcity of water has reached "critical" proportions. Moreover, most of China's rivers have by now come to suffer from substantial pollution. Chinese authorities have also expressed concern at the fact that the flow of the Yellow River is getting depleted while meeting the demands of development in western China. Since engineers conceived it in 1989, the South–North Water Project has come to be looked upon as the magic bullet. Work on it has already begun, and major works in it are certain to have been executed within the period covered by this study.

The essential objective — developed at length in the book by engineers and other officers, *Tibet's Waters Will Save China* — is to divert waters of the Tibetan plateau to the north and northwest. The project has been endorsed at several levels, including, it is reported, by the President, Hu Jintao, himself a hydrologist and former Martial Law Administrator of Tibet. Engineering work and surveys have been extensively reported to have commenced. As have parts that will eventually compose the project in its entirety: after building two dams upstream, China is now reported to be aiming to build three more dams across the Mekong; it has also commenced work on a complex of tunnels — reported to traverse over 300 kilometres eventually — that will be used for diverting the rivers that flow into India, Bangladesh and Southeast Asia.

And water is just one resource for which China and India will be in competition just as the Tibetan plateau is just one theatre in which India will have to compete with China for resources.

For all these reasons, apart from the steps that have been listed above, India must realise that:

- It cannot in the coming 20 years afford to fall behind China as it has fallen behind it during the last twenty years. It will have to do much more than it has been doing to acquire "Comprehensive National Strength".
- It must seek to make common cause with countries, especially those on the rim of China, that feel apprehensive about China's growing strength and intentions.
- It must make special efforts to develop its northeastern states as well as enter into enduring partnerships with Nepal, Bhutan and other similarly situated countries.

- It must make common cause with states along the Mekong to strengthen international conventions and treaties regarding the rights of lower riparian states.

Pakistan

We can only hope that things will change in the future but, at present, two facts stare at all who are concerned about the region: Pakistan is the singular and major source of instability, violence and terrorism in India and beyond; second, it seems set on becoming the source of even greater trouble in the foreseeable future.

It is difficult to anticipate what relations with Pakistan will be over the period covered by this study, and what the options are for a country situated next to it because it is difficult to settle on one forecast about the future of Pakistan. At present about 40 per cent of the territory of Pakistan has been wrenched out of the reach of Islamabad: Federally Administered Tribal Areas and parts of the North–West Frontier Province are now areas in which the Taliban and local extremist groups rule; these groups have driven government forces even out of the Swat Valley, an area just 100 miles from Islamabad; the groups have shown that they can now strike in Lahore, in Islamabad — that is, in the heart of Pakistan, and the strongholds of the Pakistan army itself; an insurgency has been raging in Baluchistan for the last several years; Karachi itself continues to be a tinder box. Will Pakistan's leaders, both civilian and military, have the acumen, statesmanship and vision to pull it out of the current morass? Or will the country continue on the perilous course down which it has been hurtling, and implode?

Several outcomes are equi-probable. In the face of such volatility, India's approach can only be to:

- Ensure that Pakistan does not exacerbate tensions with India — either in Kashmir or elsewhere — to divert attention domestically and internationally from what it is doing to itself and to others.
- Ensure that the blowback effect of either an increase in *jihadi* terrorism (should the Taliban succeed) or of a confrontation with the

jihadi terrorists (should the Pakistan state decide to act against them) does not impact on India.

- Prepare for a refugee influx into India in case the situation within Pakistan continues to deteriorate — either because the extremists succeed or because the economic and ecological problems, including those related to water, become more acute.

- Should Pakistan and its economy stabilise, encourage economic relations in terms of bilateral trade which can be mutually beneficial — always taking the precaution that Indian economic interests are not made hostage to developments and decisions in Pakistan. Thus, for instance, the Iran-Pakistan-India oil/gas pipeline should be kept in abeyance.

- While encouraging people-to-people contacts or the peace process, be aware of their limitations: the crucial determinant is not this ruler or that, it is the nature of the State and society of Pakistan — a state in which the army and intelligence agencies have a role that is more pervasive and triggers apprehensions of an order that outsiders can scarcely imagine; a society in which extremist notions have percolated far and wide. Given the deep and pervasive power of the army and of extremist groups and indeed of the ideology on which Pakistan has been weaned, when it comes to India, all Pakistani institutions and non-state actors take their lead from the elements whose power and position depend on perpetuating hatred towards India. Until the nature of the Pakistani state and society changes, efforts to normalise relations will continue to follow a stop-and-go course.

It is evident that the problems that Pakistan is causing India cannot be contained merely through getting it to sign some agreements and declarations — witness the fate of the commitments that Pakistan has made both bilaterally in agreements with India as well as multilaterally at the United Nations that it will not allow territory under its control to be used for terrorism against India or other countries. Nor can they be contained by local anti-terrorist operations in areas like Kashmir. What India needs is for Pakistan to act as a responsible neighbour. It is evident, however, that Pakistan will not be good neighbour unless it is forced to behave like one. Should all efforts of India towards this objective fail; should the countries which can in fact put effective pressure on Pakistan to change course refuse to use the leverage they have; should Pakistan fall even more under the sway of extremist elements and ideology, India, and indeed the international community at large, will have to strive to ensure that its disintegration is orderly.

This will entail a combination of two prongs. One will be to "do a Reagan to Pakistan" — that is, to engage it in an economic and arms race of an order that it cannot either dodge or sustain. The second would be to "do a Kashmir to Pakistan", that is to widen the earth-faults that today bedevil the country.

In a word, among its neighbours, Pakistan presents India with options that are ominous in the extreme. However, that does not make them options that the country can afford to ignore.

Bangladesh

Unlike Pakistan, Bangladesh, is more stable — at the time of writing, it has just held an election that has restored democratic governance and ended two years of military rule. However, the country has been showing worrying trends towards Islamic extremism — that the most overtly "religious" of parties lost almost all the seats it contested cannot provide lasting comfort: any more than the fact that the "religious" parties in Pakistan never got more than four per cent of the vote in national elections should have been a ground for concluding that extremism was getting contained in that country.

Over the next decade, there will be a seesaw battle within Bangladesh between democratic forces and Islamisation. Another element that will determine the outcome, and circumscribe India's options will be what happens to left-wing extremism that has begun to surface and to Bonapartist tendencies on the other.

India's interests and options *vis à vis* Bangladesh over the next 10–15 years would be to

- Ensure that the influx of illegal Bangladeshis into India is halted;
- Ensure that Islamisation trends from Bangladesh do not enter India, especially *via* Assam;
- Prevent *jihadi* terrorists, encouraged by Pakistan, from entering India through Bangladesh;
- Prevent sanctuary being given to Indian insurgent groups like ULFA in Bangladesh as well as to prevent the supply of illegal weapons to them through Bangladesh;
- Negotiate land transit through Bangladesh that will reduce the distance and cost of supplying the Northeast;
- Ensure that China does not gain overbearing influence over, that it does not come to use Bangladesh to hobble India as it has been using Pakistan;
- As a hangover from East Pakistan, influential elements within Bangladesh still look upon the Northeast as an area which must come under it as part of a larger Bangladesh. These revanchist notions have been the rationale for justifying illegal migration into Assam, as they have been the rationale for giving sanctuary to terrorist and secessionist groups like the ULFA. These notions have to be scotched lest they fester and grow into the sort of problem that the ideology of hatred that has taken hold in Pakistan constitutes for India today.

It would, of course, be an ideal outcome if India and Bangladesh could join hands to ensure development. That there are a host of opportunities around which such cooperative endeavour can be organised is evident — the development of oil and gas reserves, the production of fertilisers and other downstream products based on these is just one of several opportunities. As cooperation with India in projects of this kind seems to encounter obstacles that governments in Bangladesh have hitherto not been able to surmount — witness the fate recently of strenuous efforts by the TATAs to set up a fertiliser and steel complex within Bangladesh — two approaches are possible. One is to invite an agency like the ADB to take the matter in hand. The other is to intensify cooperation with Myanmar — both to develop its gas reserves and to secure access to India's northeast.

Sri Lanka

Just as India may at some time in the future have to contemplate a situation in which it may have to assist an orderly disintegration of Pakistan, it must assist the smaller countries around it to remain united. It is, therefore, all to the good that at long last the government of Sri Lanka is acquiring the upper hand in its struggle against the Liberation Tigers of Tamil Eelam (LTTE).

Apart from helping Sri Lanka remain whole and united, India has to ensure both that (1) the cadre and controllers of the LTTE, pressed in Sri Lanka, do not come across and set up bases within India; and that (2) there is no large-scale influx of Tamil refugees into India. Were even the latter to come back to Tamil Nadu, they, with their resentments, would become the base for the cadre to return and establish themselves. In any event, were either set to return, parochial and secessionist politics would revive in Tamil Nadu.

On the other hand, even if the LTTE is crushed today but resentments continue to fester, unrest would erupt again. Hence, to the extent feasible, it is in the interest of Sri Lanka as well as India's own interest that the latter use its considerable influence to ensure that a fair and reasonable constitutional arrangement comes to prevail in Sri Lanka so that moderate Tamils also get opportunities to fulfil their aspirations.

The troubles that have plagued Sri Lanka during the last decade, and that fact that, after the abortive Indian Peace Keeping Force Mission to assist the Sri Lankan government to thwart the LTTE, India has more or less stayed away, have led the Sri Lankan government to seek arms and assistance from Pakistan for battling the LTTE. To a lesser but significant extent, China too has been able to fish in troubled waters. To prevent these countries from entrenching themselves in the island and begin using it as yet another theatre from which to foment trouble for it, India must shed the reticence that has characterised its approach towards Sri Lanka, and become an active partner of the country in ensuring its development and security.

These are longer-term tasks. The immediate task, however, is to ensure that the ethnic conflict of Sri Lanka does not spillover into the domestic politics and life of Tamil Nadu, and thus once again stoke embers that it has taken decades to quieten.

Nepal

Nepal has been through an architectonic transformation. As recent events show, matters are far from settled: the Maoists are using the interregnum to place their cadre into the apparatus of governance; they have steadfastly refused to hand over their arms; they have also kept others uncertain about how they plan to "integrate" their 25,000 strong guerrilla force; and they have begun usurping the properties and possessions of those who they decide oppose them. Their clear aim is to establish control over the State apparatus, and, having done so, call elections by managing which they can get a clear majority on their own. The objective they are striving to attain is clear to conventional political parties as is the fact that, once they win on their own, the Maoists will snuff out all other political entities. The *Mahdesis*, the people of Indian origin along the *Terai*, too have been feeling insecure — a major movement of unrest among them has just about quietened down.

Apart from the fact that, what with open borders, an unsettled neighbour can spell trouble, three factors require close attention:

- Leftwing violence has come to affect almost a third of the districts within India itself. The victory of Maoists in Nepal naturally has boosted the morale of Naxalites in India. India must ensure that ideological affinity does not induce the Nepalese government to allow Naxalites from India to secure sanctuary in Nepal.

- Over the past 15 years, Pakistan's intelligence agencies established substantial footholds in Nepal from which they commenced anti-Indian activities — a symptom of these footholds was the sudden mushrooming of mosques and *madrasas* right across the Indo-Nepalese border even though there is little Muslim population in the areas. Were this to be allowed to grow, it will become a very substantial problem — in particular because a major proportion of the activities of Pakistani agencies, including the establishment of mosques and *madrasas*, has been focussed right at the "chicken's neck" of North Bengal, the sliver, just 30 miles wide, that connects India's northeast to the rest of India.
- That Nepal is now in the hands of Maoists naturally gives China a great opportunity to extend its influence to the southern slopes of the Himalayas.

The ferment in Nepal, therefore, will require India to pay close attention to and devote very substantial resources to Nepal. Specifically, it will have to strive to:

- Ensure that linkages do not strengthen between the Maoists of Nepal and the Maoist insurgency in India;
- Ensure a fair deal for the *Mahdesis* or people of India origin;
- Persuade the Government of Nepal not to allow Pakistani agencies to use Nepal as platform for activities hostile to India, in particular to guard against the mushrooming of mosques and *madrasas* on the Indo-Nepal border;
- Forestall the ingress of *jihadi* ideology and *jihadis* from the porous border;
- Implement a system of border documentation checks, if not passports and visas;
- As the government of Nepal will play China off against India, match Chinese efforts and resources.

As vital to India's interests is the opportunity to work with Nepal to ensure the growth and prosperity of that country. Little can repay its efforts and resources as much as partnering with Nepal to develop its hydro resources. At present the total annual budget of the Government in Kathmandu is not much more than US$1.5 billion. Were India to undertake to finance the entire budget for 30 years, and, in addition, to finance the entire cost of the hydro-electric projects of common interest, *and* earmark the quantum of electricity that Nepal would need for its own use, the cost at which it would ensure power for itself would almost certainly be less than the cost at which power would be available to it as a result of the Indo-US nuclear agreement. In addition, the benefits that would accrue in terms of controlling floods that now regularly devastate large parts of Uttar Pradesh and Bihar would be enormous. Both from a geo-strategic point of view, therefore, and from the economic point of view, assuring Nepal of the most generous terms in projects that it may agree to undertake with India would greatly be in India's interest. This is where India would be well advised to seek the help of agencies like the ADB.

The Extended Neighbourhood

South Asia and, therefore, India will also be greatly impacted by what happens in the Association of Southeast Asian Nations (ASEAN) countries to the east and by what happens in Afghanistan, Iran, and Central Asian republics in the west.

The one development from which the severest consequences can befall India is that the United States and North Atlantic Treaty Organisation forces retreat in defeat from Afghanistan. Apart from once again extending the hold of Pakistan to an area that can be used to incubate terrorists, such retreat will give a huge boost to Islamic fundamentalism. The victory will at once multiply manifold the chances of Pakistan itself falling to the fundamentalists. Only with considerable difficulty will its votaries be able to get at the United States, and then too only for the stand-alone 9/11 type attack. They will be able to get at European nations with lesser difficulty — as Europe has a substantial enough population of Islamic origin that a few among it will be disposed to provide local help and recruits; and, even more so, because many of its governments are still hobbled by political correctness. They will almost certainly target a few regimes in the Middle East. But the easiest target for them will be a soft and slip-shod State like India. For all these reasons, every step that India can take to shore up a non-extremist regime in Afghanistan will be in its interest.

The same holds for the Central Asian republics. India has had good ties with them. It enjoys good repute among them — both for goodwill towards them as well as for competence. It already has a small presence in the form of an airbase in Tajikistan. The countries realise that they share several common concerns with India, including that of preventing Afghanistan from being taken over by extremist elements. The enormous strides that China has made in the region — its announced plans to invest US$100 billion in the region; the exploration rights it has secured in 40 per cent of Kazakhstan; the pipeline it is building to ferry oil from the region; the platform China has constructed in the Shanghai Cooperation Organization; the fact that because of its circumstances, Russia is not able to be an effective counter to China in this vital region — are yet another reason for India to pay close attention and devote resources to Central Asia over the coming twenty years.

For the same sorts of reasons, and also because of India's dependence on imported oil and gas, the Middle East will continue to require attention. There is the additional reason that the region remains a tinderbox. Indeed, every indicator suggests that instability and uncertainties in the region and emanating from it will intensify. Will Iran not acquire nuclear weapons? Once it does so, can its neighbours — in particular, Saudi Arabia, Egypt and Turkey — desist from doing so? The former two are known to have had undeclared nuclear programmes for long. Similarly, Iran has already been able to extend its reach through the Hezbollah in Lebanon, the Hamas in Palestine, and the Mahdists in Iraq: how will it use these instruments in the coming decades? And what will happen to relative power balances in the region when the Americans withdraw from Iraq? The turn that each of these uncertainties takes will have major consequences for India in the coming decades. However, we cannot pursue the possibilities here without going far beyond the remit of this study.

General Observations

Four general observations deserve to be repeated as we conclude this brief survey.

First, India will have to pay much greater attention, devote much greater resources to foreign affairs than it has hitherto. And for the first time in 60 years, it now has the wherewithal to do so. Along with deploying resources, India will have to learn to harness all limbs of policy — from granting facilities to foreign firms to set up operations in India to the stance it takes in trade negotiations to the strategic partnerships it enters into — towards common objectives. Practical, concrete steps, real resources, and not pronouncements and postures in international conferences — that is the reorientation that India will have to execute.

Second, as even this chapter shows, the tasks are of such an order, the problems are so intertwined, that no country can address all of them on its own. Like other countries, India will have to forge alliances for each of them.

Different issues will call for different associates. South Korea, Japan, Taiwan, Vietnam, Australia, the United States for dealing with China; China, Japan — a major donor to the country — Russia, the United States, Saudi Arabia to exchange possibilities regarding Pakistan; these countries as well as Israel and Turkey to exhume and uproot fundamentalist ideology and Iran and Russia in regard to Central Asia... In a word, nimbleness.

Third, India's immediate neighbours present many opportunities as well as challenges. To approach them, India must, among other things, deepen its relations with countries beyond them — with the Central Asian republics on the one hand, and those in ASEAN on the other.

However, all this is contingent on one overriding imperative, the *sine qua non*. India has to do well at home in all spheres and at all levels.

It has to acquire "Comprehensive National Strength". As the Gurus have said:

> *Bal chchutkyo bandhan pade, kachchu na hot upaaye*
> *Kahe Nanak ab toh Hari gaj jyon ho sahaaye*
>
> *Bal howa bandhan kate, sabhi kich hot upaaye*
> *Nanak sab kuch tumhre haat mein tumhi he ho sahaaye*[2]

---

[2] The translation for this passage is:
If your strength is frittered away, and nothing can be done, Nanak says now we must go into God's shelter for help.
If there is strength, it will remove constraints, and anything can be done.
Nanak says that everything is in your hands, you are the only saviour.

Chapter 2

South Asia: Economic Outlook in the Next Few Decades

Shahid Javed Burki

Introduction

There is an emerging consensus among economists — in particular those that watch and analyse global trends — that the center of gravity of the global economy has begun to shift towards the emerging world. A couple of estimates illustrate this well. The International Monetary Fund (IMF) is of the view that the combined output of America, Europe and Japan is likely to contract by 0.1 per cent in 2009. The deepening recession in these countries — mostly the result of the financial crisis that surfaced in the summer of 2007 in America and spread to other shores — now engulfs Europe and has begun to have an impact on Japan. The emerging world was expected to escape the consequences of this crisis as its financial system was not as well integrated with the global structure. But even this part of the world was not spared. Even the rapidly growing economies of China, Brazil and India will see some reduction in the rate of increase in their Gross Domestic Product (GDP). Nonetheless, the World Bank estimates that the combined output of the emerging world will increase by 4.5 per cent in 2009. Juxtaposing these two estimates, that for the combined GDP of the industrial countries and the emerging world, suggests that in 2009, emerging countries will be responsible for 100 per cent of the increase in global output.

Another set of numbers suggest that whereas the emerging world today accounts for 35 per cent of global product, this is likely to increase to 50 per cent in 15 years time. If the present trends continue,

Table 1:   Distribution of the global product and population

	Population		Surface Area		Gross National Income		Gross National Income (PPP)	
	Millions	%	Thousand	%	$ billion	%	$ billion	%
Low income	2,352	36.5	29,265	21.8	1,377	3.1	5,849	9.6
Middle income	3,074	47.7	70,081	52.3	8,138	18.0	22,137	36.0
High income	1,011	15.7	34,595	25.8	35,643	78.9	32,900	54.0
World	6,438		144,941		45,158	100.0	60,670	

Source: The World Bank, *World Development Indicators 2007*, Washington DC, 2007, Table 1.1, pp. 14–16.

by 2030, the emerging world will account for more than one half of the global GDP. However, the emerging world encompasses a very large area and counts the vast proportion of the world's population as its citizenry. As shown in Table 1, if we define emerging markets as those that fall in the World Bank's middle income category then in 2005 they had a share of 48 per cent in world population and 37 per cent in world product measured in purchasing power parity terms. As against this the poorer parts of the world — most of them in Sub-Saharan Africa — had 37 per cent of the world's population but only three per cent of the global product.

The question I would like to ask concerns the future of South Asia in the anticipated shifts in the global economy. If the centre of gravity of the global economy were to shift towards the emerging world, would this also include South Asia? Before answering this question, it would be useful to provide a quick overview of the South Asian position in the global economy and how the various countries in the region relate with one another. For this, we turn to the numbers provided in Table 2. We define South Asia to include India, Pakistan, Bangladesh, Nepal and Sri Lanka listed in terms of their population. In 2005, the region had a population of 1.44 billion. The non-South Asian emerging world had a population of 1.63 billion, 13 per cent higher than South Asia's. However, in terms of the combined incomes of the South Asian countries, their share was slightly more than one-quarter,

Table 2: The economies of South Asia

	Population		Gross National Income		Gross National Income (PPP)		Per Capita Income
	Millions	%	Billion	%	Million	%	
India	1,095	76.0	804	79.8	3,187	82.5	3,458
Pakistan	156	10.8	107	10.6	366	8.0	2,346
Bangladesh	142	9.9	67	6.6	296	6.5	2,085
Sri Lanka	20	1.4	23	2.3	89	1.9	4,450
Nepal	27	1.9	7	0.7	42	0.0	1,556
	1,440	100	1,008	100.0	4,588	99.9	3,186

Source: See Table 1.

26.1 per cent of the combined GDP of all emerging economies. With combined income of US$4.6 trillion, the South Asian region was economically much smaller than the non-South Asian emerging markets that had a combined income of US$17.5 trillion.

Non-South Asian emerging markets' share in global output was 28.9 per cent compared to only eight per cent for the South Asian region. The South Asia per capita income was only US$ 3,186 compared to US$10,740 for the non-South Asian emerging markets. What these numbers suggest is that while it may be legitimate to count the countries of South Asia among emerging markets, they still lag considerably behind the rest of the emerging world which is made up of the countries in East Asia, Latin America, North Africa and South and Central Europe.

With this as the background, I will turn to an analysis of the economic situation in South Asia. I will divide the discussion that follows into three parts. In the first, I will provide a quick overview of the performance of this part of the world in the 40 year period between the time the region gained independence (in the late 1940s) to the mid-1980s when India, followed by Pakistan and Bangladesh a couple of years later, began to reform their economies. The second part will provide a brief analysis of the current situation in South Asia while the third part will look into the future and indicate how South Asia is likely to fare in the next couple of decades as the global economy gets to be restructured in several different ways.

South Asia: 1947–1986

When the British left India, they handed South Asia to three different governments — India, Pakistan and Sri Lanka. Of these India and Sri Lanka had been separate administrative and political entities even under colonial rule. Pakistan was a new country, carved out of British India to provide a separate homeland for the Muslim community of the area. The Muslims, led by Muhammad Ali Jinnah, had successfully argued that they should be treated as a separate nation, deserving of its own state. This was granted but with some reluctance, especially by the leaderships that dominated the first few administrations of India. Jawaharlal Nehru, who was to remain as India's prime minister for 17 years was particularly hostile to the idea of Pakistan:[1] that the Muslims could not flourish in a multi-religious, multi-cultural, and multi-lingual India that he wished to create. For him that was to be the "idea of India".[2] This conflict between the two ideas was to have a profound impact on Pakistan's early economic history. Pakistan had to start with a clean state; it had to create a new government, locate it in a new capital and redefine the structure of its two largest provinces — Bengal in the east and Punjab in the west — which too were partitioned on the basis of religion. With the government just starting to function and the instruments of the state very weak, the first generation of Pakistani leaders left the task of developing the economy in the hands of the private sector. There was these two different approaches followed by the two major economies of South Asia. While India inspired by the Soviet Union, placed the public sector on the commanding heights of the economy Pakistan placed its trust in private enterprise. India used the state to influence resource

---

[1] Stephen Philip Cohen, *The Idea of Pakistan*, New Delhi, Oxford University Press, 2004.
[2] See Sunil Khilnani, *The Idea of India*, New York, Farrar, Straus and Giroux, 1998.

allocation even by the state sector using what came to be known as the "license raj". In Pakistan a much more underdeveloped state allowed greater deal of operational freedom to the private sector.

These different approaches resulted in different performances for the economy. For nearly four decades after gaining independence, the average Indian GDP growth rate hovered around 3.5 per cent a year while the Pakistani economy grew at a rate about two percentage points. The low Indian GDP increase was dubbed as the Hindu rate of growths by Raj Krishna, notable Indian economist while Pakistan's much better performance was celebrated by a number of development economists, including Harvard University's Gustav F. Papanek,[3] as the consequence of a model of growth for other countries. The most important element of the Pakistani model was its focus on growth and disregard of poverty alleviation and income distribution as appropriate objectives of public policy.[4] These goals would be met by what was called the "trickle down" consequence of rapid economic growth.

A two percentage growth premium that Pakistan had enjoyed over India in the 40 year period between independence and the mid-eighties meant that while the size of its economy increased almost six fold, that of India grew four-fold. By the mid-1980s, Pakistan had not only closed the economic gap that existed in 1947, its income per capita overtook that of India.

However, this trend did not continue largely because of the changes in the direction of public policy in both countries. After Prime Minister Zulfikar Ali Bhutto assumed power in December 1971, he undertook a programme of nationalisation that brought not only large scale industries and financial institutions under the control of the state. The government also nationalised small agro-based industries as well as privately-run colleges. The role of the state expanded enormously. In one stroke, Pakistan had adopted the Indian model of growth and economic management by putting the state at the centre of the

---

[3] Gustav F. Papanek, *Pakistan's Development*, Cambridge Mass, Harvard University, 1967.

[4] See for instance Mahbub ul Haq, *Strategy of Economic Planning: A Case Study of Pakistan*, Karachi Oxford University Press, 1967.

economy. The immediate consequence of this change in direction was to reduce the rate of economic growth.

In the late 1980s, the Indians changed the role of the state, allowing much greater space to the private sector. This process gathered pace after 1981 when Manmohan Singh, as Finance Minister, had to face a severe economic crisis produced by a widening trade gap. His team of economic managers decided to demolish the "license raj" and to allow the private sector to trust its own instincts. Some controls still remained, especially those on the labour markets. The government did not liberate the financial sector. Foreign direct investment (FDI) was also encouraged and the level of tariffs were significantly reduced. The economy responded immediately to these changes; by the end of the decade, the Indian economy was expanding at the rates more than twice the historical average. These reforms spelled a paradigm shift in the Indian development model.

No such shift occurred in Pakistan. Mostly because of extreme political instability after the death of President Zia ul Haq, the country's third military President, there were frequent changes in government. In the 11-year period between 1988 and 1999, the country was governed by four elected administrations and four caretaker administrations. There was no continuity in the direction of economic policy as each administration developed its own approach. Pakistan fell steadily behind India. As shown in Table 2, Pakistan's income per head where measured in purchasing power parity terms was only 68 per cent that of India's in 2005. India's GDP growth was almost twice as high as that of Pakistan in the two decades between the mid-1980s and the present.

The Present Situation in South Asia

The remarkable economic performance of India over the last two decades has not placed it on the some trajectory of economic change and development as the one on which China and other East Asian economies are moving. At the same time, Pakistan is not on the trajectory India has followed in the past 20 years. The reasons for these are structural. Structurally, India is as different from the

East Asian economies as Pakistan is from India. The foundations on which the East Asian have built their economies are different from those on which the Indians have erected the structure of their economy. These are shaky compared to those of East Asia. They are shakier still in Pakistan.

The East Asian economic success is based on a number of factors. Four of these are worth emphasising. The first is enormous investment in human development. The East Asians, the Chinese included, have much better educated and trained work-force than do the Indians. Second, in spite of the recent increases in income inequality in China, the East Asians started on the path of economic progress with much better equity in the distribution of economic assets. Consequently, the fruits of growth were more equally shared than was the case in India. Third, the East Asian economies were much more open than those of South Asia which resulted in their better integration in the global economic system. As the structure of the global economy changed, the process of globalisation that made it happen provided benefits to the South Asian economies. Both India and Pakistan remained more closed and less well integrated in the global economy than the East Asians. Fourth, the East Asians have savings rates much higher than those in South Asia which has made them less dependent on external capital flows than was the case for the economies of South Asia. That notwithstanding, as shown in Table 3, the South Asians, with the exception of Pakistan and Sri Lanka, have begun to approach the levels achieved by the East Asians in the mid-1990s. Bangladesh doubled its savings rate in this period, while India increased its by 10 percentage points. The Indian rate, however, is still well below that of China but is equal to that of Korea and is approaching that of Malaysia.

Not only these differences mark the development models pursued by the two regions. It would be useful to mention two other features of the South Asian economies which would in all probability affect their future performance. Rapid development in South Asia, whenever it has occurred, remained concentrated in a few geographical areas and was led by a few sectors that further contributed to the growth of general and regional disparities. In the case of India, the

Table 3:   Saving ratios in East and South Asia

	% of GDP	
	1990	2005
East Asia		
China	40	51
Indonesia	28	24
Korea	37	32
Malaysia	30	36
Singapore	46	—
Thailand	33	29
South Asia		
Bangladesh	14	30
India	22	32
Nepal	11	31
Pakistan	22	18
Sri Lanka	17	20

Source: The World Bank, *World Development Indicators 2007*, Table 4.8, pp. 218–220.

states along the Western coast and in the south have led recent growth. Growth was also led by the service sector — information technology and health services in particular — than by the economy traditional sectors. This has resulted in significant inequality among the regions of the country and its citizenry. In spite of the rapid economic growth the country has experienced in recent years, a significant proportion of Indians continue to live in absolute poverty. The proportion is much higher than that for any of the East Asian countries.

Pakistan has even more structural problems than its neighbour. Four of these need to be highlighted. First, the country has the lowest savings rate among the major economies of Asia; as shown in Table 3, it is significantly lower than other countries of South Asia. What is worrying is that the rate is declining. In the 15-year period between 1990 and 2005, the savings rate fell by 4 percentage points. Second, the country has not paid much attention to developing its large and growing human resource. Pakistan started its existence as an independent state with a population of 32 million. Sixty one years later, the population has increased more than five fold to reach 165 million. Because of the high rates of growth in the decades between 1960 and 1990, the median age of the population is low, only 17 years. This means that the country has more than 80 million people below the age of 17. Neglected in terms of its social development, such a population can become a serious burden on the economy and the society. Properly educated and trained, it can become an economic asset. The latter has happened in the case of the countries of East Asia, in particular, China. Even India which has not invested as much in human development as have the countries of East Asia, has pockets of well educated and trained people. These have contributed to the remarkable development of the Indian information technology and health sectors. In turn, as discussed above, these sectors have contributed to the rapid growth in recent decades of the Indian economy.

Today, Pakistan spends less than two per cent of its GDP on education provided by the public sector. This is one of the lowest ratios in the world. This is one reason why the economy remained technologically backward and has a poor future if the state does not change its priorities.

The third structural weakness in the economy is that it does not produce enough exportable surpluses. As shown in Table 4, not only is the share of exports in GDP low relative to other Asian economies; over the last 15 years, the GDP growth rate has outstripped the rate of increase by half a percentage point. Pakistan is the only country in Asia which this has happened. Unless the country focuses on developing exports, it will continues experience the kind of balance of payments crisis it faces at this time and far which it had to go to the IMF to find some relief.

The fourth weakness lies in the domain of politics and institutions. Largely because of the periodic interventions by the military in politics, the Pakistani political system has become highly centralised. Although the constitution adopted in 1973 provided for a federal system, the promises made to the smaller province were not kept. Consequently, Islamabad is all powerful with little authority wielded

Table 4:   Trade and foreign direct investment

Countries	Trade as % of GDP		Growth in Trade Loss Growth in Real GDP	FDI as % of GDP	
	1990	2005	1990–2005	1990	2005
Bangladesh	17.6	38.5	4.2	0	13.4
India	13.1	28.5	4.4	0.1	0.8
Nepal	24.1	36.1	—	3.5	6.5
Pakistan	32.6	37.3	−0.5	0.6	2.0
Sri Lanka	57.3	64.7	2.5	0.5	1.2
China	32.5	63.6	6.3	1.0	3.5
Korea	51.1	69.3	6.4	0.3	0.6
Malaysia	133.4	196.1	2.9	5.3	3.0

Source: The World Bank, *World Development Indicators 2007*, Washington DC, Table 6.1, pp. 316–318.

by the provinces. This has created a large distance between the citizenry and those who govern.

South Asia's Economic Future

The past and the present are the only guides to the future. What happens to the economies of South Asia will depend more on domestic public policies the countries adopt. The external environment will also play a role but not as much as in the case for the more globally integrated economies of East Asia.

Based on what has already happened, I can make the following five predictions about the region. One, the South Asia region will expand at rates between six to eight per cent a year in the next decade out a half, say upto the year 2025. The higher rate will be possible only if domestic polices support growth, poverty alleviation and improvements in income distribution. Relations between the countries of the region will also play an important role in particular in increasing trade. Pakistan's ability to control the rise in extremism will also be an important factor. With a six per cent increase in out, the size of the GDP will increase more than two

Table 5: Trade, balance of payments and fiscal balances

| Countries | Trade Balance Latest 12 Months ($ billion) | Current Account Balance | | Budget Balance % of GDP 2008 |
		Latest 12 Months	% of GDP 2008	
China	265.2	371.8	+8.5	−2.0
Indonesia	17.3	6.3	+2.8	4.3
Korea	−12.2	−10.6	−3.3	1.1
Malaysia	41.9	35.3	13.7	−4.8
Thailand	3.7	5.4	+1.1	+1.1
India	106.5	−21.9	−2.9	−4.3
Pakistan	−22.4	−14.0	−6.2	−6.7

Source: The Economist, 27 November 2008, p. 118. Accessible at http://www.economist.com/markets/indicators/displaystory.cfm?story_id=12689914.

and a half times and income per head of the population will more than double.

Two, democracy will throw deeper roots in the region, in both Bangladesh and Pakistan. The political system in Pakistan will allow for greater decentralisation with more economic decision-making authority allowed to the provinces. In that respect, the system will, begin to resemble the one that has been evolving in India.

Third, South Asia will continue to have large pockets of poverty. With the population increasing by a third between 2005 and 2025 reaching two billion by the latter year, there will still be about 400 million people living in absolute poverty. It has been difficult to address the problem poverty because the power wielded by powerful elites in the political system.

Fourth, the extent of participation in the global system will be less than that achieved by the East Asian economies. In spite of the effort to open the economies that began in the early 1990s, the region remains relatively close to trade, capital flows, in particular; FDI. India, for instance, has fairly shift regulations of foreign participation in various sectors of the economy. This is largely because of the collective power of the players in these sectors. Labour is reluctant to allow free movement of worker with the country and small retailers wield enough political power to block the entry of large marketing conglomerates into the country.

Fifth, and more positively, we will see greater integration of the regional economics. The South Asian Free Trade Area, inaugurated with such fanfare and enthusiasm at the South Asian Association for Regional Cooperation Summit held in Islamabad in January 2004 has not made much progress in bringing together the countries of the region. This may change as regionalism replaces nationalism among the new generation of South Asian leaders.

Chapter 3

Integrating with the World: South Asia Rising — Enhancing Trade and Investment

Saman Kelegama

Introduction

Most South Asian countries started to open up and integrate with global economies in the late 1980s. They showed high growth rates after they opened up their economies and embarked on deeper integration with the global economy. Vigorous growth of South Asia has been accompanied by their more vigorous participation in international trade. The increase in trade and investment followed the open economic policy regimes.

Unilateral liberalisation took place in Sri Lanka first in 1977, followed by Bangladesh in 1987, Pakistan in 1988, and India in 1991.[1] Maldives had a more or less an open economy and Bhutan is a closely integrated economy to India. Since opening up, trade dependence ratio of all South Asian countries have increased and shown an increasing trend over the years (Table 1). After experiencing the open economy for more than a decade, all South Asian countries showed very high growth of exports and imports (Tables 2 and 3).

Trade performance improved remarkably since 2002. Average growth of exports of South Asia during 2002/08 was 19.3 per cent, compared to 5.3 per cent during the previous five years. Average growth of exports of the world during 2002–08 was 11 per cent

---

[1] For a survey, see Chowdhury and Mahmud (2008).

Table 1:   Trade dependence of South Asian Countires

Year	Bangladesh	India	Pakistan	Sri Lanka
1985–87	18.3	13.8	35.6	61.7
1990–92	20.1	19.0	42.4	67.9
1996–98	30.9	25.2	37.7	79.2
2000–02	35.0	28.5	32.3	84.0
2006	45.1	32.4	37.0	63.6

Source: ADB (2008); RIS (2008).

Table 2:   Average export growth rate of South Asia (%)

	South Asia	India	Pakistan	Bangladesh
Avg (1997–2001)	5.3	5.9	1.8	10.7
Avg (2002–2008)	19.3	28.3	20.3	11.5

Source: ADB (2008); RIS (2008).

Table 3:   Average import growth rate of South Asia (%)

	South Asia	India	Pakistan	Bangladesh
Avg (1997–2001)	2.2	3.6	−3.1	0.8
Avg (2002–2008)	24.6	28.8	18.7	33.2

Source: ADB (2008); RIS (2008).

compared to 3.4 per cent the previous five years. Export growth was shared by all South Asia countries, as shown in Table 4.

Manufactured goods account for bulk of the exports in all South Asian countries (Table 5). The main labour-intensive products are: textile and clothing, leather products, and footwear. The main skill-intensive products are: pharmaceuticals, cut diamonds, and automobiles. There were a few tech-intensive products also.

This chapter attempts to have a closer look at this growth in trade and some of the broad contours surrounding this growth. It highlights areas that contribute to overall rise of South Asia and how to sustain this process over the long run. No attempt is made to undertake a rigorous analysis of the factors determining the growth in trade.

Table 4: Export growth rates in South Asian Countries

	India	Pakistan	Sri Lanka	Bangladesh	South Asia
2002	20.3	2.3	−2.4	−7.6	13.6
2003	24.1	20.1	9.2	9.5	20.8
2004	48.6	20.0	12.2	15.9	24.0
2005	32.1	37.8	10.2	14.0	21.0
2006	21.8	33.3	8.5	21.5	20.1
2007	23.1	8.0	12.5	15.8	16.2
2008(P)	22.0	13.0	8.0	12.0	14.5

Source: ADB (2008); RIS (2008).

Table 5: Manufactured exports in South Asian Countries total exports (%)

	1991	2006
India	72.0	70.0
Pakistan	79.0	81.0
Bangladesh	79.8	92.0
Sri Lanka	61.6	70.0

Source: ADB (2008); RIS (2008).

The rest of the chapter is divided as follows. The second section highlights India's trade performance as a major contributor to the overall South Asian trade performance. The third section highlights foreign direct investment (FDI) inflows and outflows from South Asia with special emphasis on India. Section 4 presents the case for deepening regional integration in South Asia to benefit from India's high growth. The final section has some concluding remarks.

India's Trade Performance

When focusing on South Asia, it is India that attracts attention. India is the fourth largest economy of the world and it has the world's largest population of young people (600 million people under the age of 25 years) and a thriving middle class (Dossani, 2007). India got out of the so-called 'Hindu rate of growth' after the partial liberalisation of the economy in the mid-1980s (Nath, 2007). India's recent achievements, as documented by Panagariya (2008), is given in Box 1.

Box 1:   India's recent economic achievements

- In real dollars, the GDP grew by 13.8 per cent per annum during 2003–04 to 2005–06. In 2006–07, this growth rate was even higher.
- Merchandise exports in current dollars were $18.1 billion in 1990–91 and doubled for the first time in 1999–2000. In the recent times, they doubled in just three years: from $52.7 billion in 2002–03 to $102.7 billion in 2005–06.
- Services exports doubled from $26.9 billion in 2003–04 to $60.6 billion in 2005–06.
- India is now far more integrated into the world economy than in 1990. The exports of goods and services as a proportion of the GDP rose from 7.2 per cent in 1990–91 to 11.6 per cent in 1999–2000, and shot up to 20.5 per cent in 2005–06. The proportion of total trade to the GDP reached 43.1 per cent in 2005–06.
- Total foreign investment rose from $6 billion in 2002–03 to $20.2 billion in 2005–06, and shot up to $16.4 billion in the first ten months of 2006–07.
- Remittances rose from $17.2 billion in 2002–03 to $24.6 billion in 2005–06.
- As of April 7, 2007, the foreign exchange reserves crossed the $200 billion mark.
- There has been a revolution in the telecommunications sector. For example, in 1990–91, India had approximately 5 million phone lines in total. Currently, India is adding more than 5 million phone lines per month.
- The sales of passenger vehicles rose from 707,000 in 2002–03 to 1.14 million in 2005–06. The total number of vehicles produced during 2003–06 exceeded the entire stock of registered vehicles in 1990–91.
- India's share in World exports which was 0.5 per cent in the mid-1980s increased to 1 per cent by 2005.

Source: Panagariya (2008).

Since the mid-1980s, India's exports have grown faster than global exports. Between 1990 to 2000, world merchandise exports grew annually at a rate of six per cent whereas India's exports grew at 9.3 per cent. A significant transformation was realised in the new millennium as merchandise exports from India grew at a rate more than 20 per cent per annum after 2002/03. In value terms, merchandise exports trebled from US$44.7 billion in 2001/02 to US$128 billion in 2006/07. Exports as a share of gross domestic product (GDP) increased from 9.4 per cent in 2001/02 to 14 per cent in 2006/07.

Imports have grown faster than exports — in value terms they increased from US$56.2 billion in 2001/02 to US$191.2 billion in 2006/07. As a percentage of GDP, all imports registered an increase from 11.8 per cent to 20.9 per cent of GDP between 2000/02 and 2006/07. This high growth in both exports and imports was experienced in spite of the fact that the World Trade Organisation-Doha Round of trade negotiations did not result in significant trade liberalisation at the multilateral level.

Services is the largest sector in South Asian economies. The trade in the service sector in South Asia grew at 16.1 per cent during 1991–2006, surpassing the growth recorded by trade in goods (12.7 per cent). Here again, it is India that has taken the lead in growth. Services exports of India have shown the most impressive growth in recent years.

The growth of the Indian service sector was one of the key factors that contributed to India becoming a fast growing economy. The growth in services has not been confined to the domestic market but also to the external market. India's share in global trade in commercial services increased from one per cent in 1999 to 2.7 per cent in 2006. Although India's ranking in global merchandise exports was 28 in 2006, its ranking in global commercial services exports was 10 in 2006.

Table 6 shows that growth in services exports of India in the recent years has surpassed all other South Asian countries. Among developing countries, only China is ahead of India in the export of commercial services. Another noteworthy feature is that India has a significant trade surplus in commercial services, which amounted to US$10 billion in 2006 — a remarkable achievement in a short period.

Table 6:   Growth rates of South Asian Countries trade in services

	Exports	Imports
Bangladesh	8.0	7.8
India	19.1	15.8
Pakistan	5.8	9.1
Sri Lanka	8.5	8.6
South Asia	16.5	13.9

Source: ADB (2008); RIS (2008).

Table 7:   South Asian Countries structure of services exports

	India	Pakistan
Transport		
1991	19.2	62.4
2006	10.2	49.6
Travel		
1991	37.5	12.5
2006	11.9	11.3
ICT		
1991	40.4	24.3
2006	73.7	35.4
Finance/Insurance		
1991	2.2	0.8
2006	4.2	3.7

Source: ADB (2008); RIS (2008).

Seventeen services, communications and other services dominate services exports from India. For instance, Bharti Airtel is the third largest mobile telecommunication company in the world. India has emerged as a global hub for out-sourcing information communication technology (ICT) software and Business Process Outsourcing (BPO) services. India's exports of IT services amounted to US$40.4 billion in 2007/08 (Table 7). In terms of Global Service Location Index completed by AT Kearney, India occupied the first position among different countries (RIS, 2008).

Table 8: Emerging patterns of comparative advantage and complementarity in services

Category of Services	Sector	Countries with Revealed Comparative Advantage (RCA > 1)
Labour and resource intensive	Transport	Sri Lanka, Pakistan
Labour and resource intensive	Travel	Maldives, Nepal
Labour intensive	Construction	Sri Lanka
Skill and technology intensive	Communications	Bangladesh, India, Nepal, Pakistan, Sri Lanka
Skill and technology intensive	Computer and information services	India, Sri Lanka
Skill and technology intensive	Financial and insurance services	Sri Lanka

Source: ADB (2008); RIS (2008).

Other South Asian countries have not been able to exploit the potential in trade in services commensurate with their role in their economies, however, they do possess a comparative advantage in various services (Table 8). The emergence of India as a major hub for exports of software and BPO services generates opportunities for other South Asian countries in sub-contracting, expanding and later exporting such services (Hamid, 2007).

Labour migration is an important issue for India, as well as for other South Asian countries. India is gradually attracting overseas visitors in a number of ways. Tourist arrivals have been on the increase over the past decade through such promotional programme as "Incredible India" and has drawn 12 million tourists per annum. It has also been attracting global players in ICT. Thirdly, it is a low-cost service provider, attracting foreign students for higher education in such institutions as Indian Institute of Technology, Indian Institute of Management, etc., and attracting patients from around the world for relatively cheap medical care (Apollo, Escorts, etc.). Table 9 clearly indicates India's cost advantages in various types of medical care.

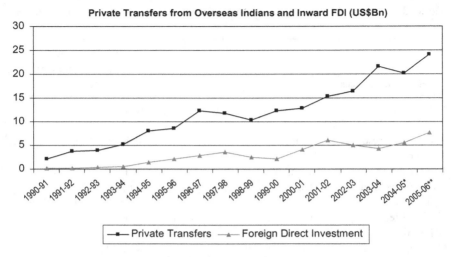

Figure 1:   Labour mobility from South Asia

Table 9:   Cost comparison of medical services

Procedure	Cost (US$)			
	USA	Thailand	India	UK
Heart Surgery	40,000	7,500	6,000	23,000
Bone Marrow Transplant	2,50,000	—	26,000	1,50,000
Liver Transplant	3,00,000	—	69,000	2,00,000
Knee Replacement	20,000	8,000	6,000	12,000
Cosmetic Surgery	20,000	3,500	2,000	10,000

Source: Escorts Heart Institute and Research Centre Limited, New Delhi.

India's exports of IT services has increased from US$4 billion in 2000 to US$40.4 billion in 2007/08. India now engages in high value specialised services — bio-information, drug testing, pharmaceutical research, engineering design and financial analysis. The cost of a call centre per annum in India is US$3,000 compared to US$25,000 per annum in the United States. India's strength in services (both in the domestic and external market) has propelled it to take a leading role in trade in services in the World Trade Organisation. Modes 1 and 4 are the strengths of India and other South Asian countries

Table 10: Private transfers from overseas Indians and inward FDI (US$Bn)

Year	Private Transfers	Foreign Direct Investment	Percent GDP
1990–91	2.06	0.09	0.7
1995–96	8.50	2.14	3.22
1999–00	12.25	2.16	2.72
2000–01	12.85	4.03	2.84
2001–02	15.39	6.12	3.29
2002–03	16.38	5.03	3.39
2003–04	21.60	4.32	3.69
2004–05*	20.25	5.58	3.03
2005–06**	24.09	7.69	3.10

Notes: *Partially Revised; **Preliminary Estimates.
Source: Compiled from Handbook of Statistics on Indian Economy, 2006, Reserve Bank of India.

and India has made many proposals on Mode 4 at the WTO. India now identifies itself with the global powers in trade in services.

FDI Inflows

FDI inflows to South Asia have grown from US$6.7 billion in the early years of the current decade to US$22 billion in 2006/07. In India, FDI flows increased from US$4.3 billion in 2003/04 to US$17 billion in 2006/07. In Pakistan, FDI inflows increased from US$0.53 billion in 2003/04 to US$4.3 billion in 2006/07. FDI flows to Sri Lanka increased from US$200 million in 2003/04 to US$480 million in 2006/07.

South Asia's share of FDI among developing countries is only three per cent and only five per cent among developing Asia. It is not much, but is certainly on the increase. Most FDI flows to South Asia are concentrated in the manufacturing and services sectors. As a percentage of gross fixed capital formation, FDI amounts to about five per cent in South Asia — not as high as in the other developing countries in Asia (which ranges from 8–25 per cent). All South Asian countries have considerably liberalized their FDI regime considerably in the last decade — FDI Confidence Index (as published by the AT Kearney Report) has improved for South Asia in recent years.

The United Nations Conference on Trade and Development reports that nearly US$10 billion of outward FDI inflows originate from South Asia (US$9.67 billion originates from India). Indian companies involved in large cross border acquisitions include:

Tata Steel   —   Corus, Hindalco — Novelis
Tata Motors   —   Jaguar Land Rover

A number of developing countries have started to look up to India as a source of FDI in recent years. For example, in 2005/06, Indian outward FDI amounted to US$5 billion, and it has increased to US$12.8 billion in 2007/08. The emergence of India as a source of 'outward investment' is impressive, given its level of development.

In many South Asian countries, FDI inflows could have been greater if there had been greater political stability and less bureaucratic obstacles. Today, in many South Asian countries, overseas remittances far outweigh FDI. This could be seen from the largest global recipient of overseas remittances, India (Figure 2).

Outward FDI from India increased from US$5 billion in 2005/06 to US$12.8 billion in 2007/08. Neigbouring South Asian countries are increasingly looking to India as a source of FDI. India is the 3rd largest FDI source for Sri Lanka (Indian Oil, Tata, Apollo, CEAT, etc.). Out of the US$10 billion, FDI outflows from South Asian countries US$9.7 billion originates from India. Sri Lanka's FDI is mainly in Maldives (hotels), followed by Bangladesh (banks and industry) and India (hotels, and a few industries). Indian companies are involved in large cross-border FDI, for instance, Tata

Table 11:   FDI inflow to the South Asian countries (US$ million)

	2003–04	2004–05	2005–06	2006–07
India	4,323	5,771	6,676	16,881
Pakistan	534	1,118	2,201	4,273
Bangladesh	350	460	692	625
Sri Lanka	229	233	272	480

Source: RIS (2008).

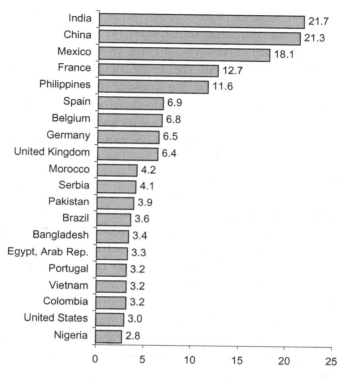

Figure 2: Top 20 remittance-recipient countries, 2004

Source: World Bank.

purchasing Tetly, Tata Motors purchasing Jaguar/Land Rover, Tata Steel purchasing Corus, Hindalco-Novelis.

Need for Regional Economic Integration

Although individually, each South Asian country has done reasonably well on growth, the contribution from South Asian regional integration to growth has not been significant. There are opportunities for a 'win-win' cooperation in the region, which still remains unexploited. The existing pattern of intra-regional trade in South Asia has failed to capture the extent of complementarities in the region, due to high incidence of non-tariff barriers (NTBs) and informal trade. Research and Information System (RIS) (2008) argues that three-fourth of intra-regional trade potential remains to be exploited. The South Asian Free Trade Area (SAFTA) can hope to realise this by assisting to create supply capacities in the lesser developed countries, and regional economic integration can provide new opportunities for trade creation and to foster equitable development. This will take place by a process of efficiency-seeking industrial restructuring that involves building production and supply capacities in relatively less developed countries through intra-regional investment.

The investment-trade nexus is yet to be exploited in the region. Where such potential can be seen is in the case of Indian investment induced trade from Sri Lanka to India under the India–Sri Lanka bilateral free trade agreement (FTA). The South Asian region has still not exploited the potential for intra-regional FDI inflows, especially with Indian companies undertaking relatively large investments in different parts of the world. Of course, to reap investment benefits under the SAFTA, the South Asian countries should remove NTBs and reduce the 'negative list'. Furthermore, Pakistan's imports from India are still governed by the positive list as Pakistan has not provided Most-Favoured Nation treatment to India. Thus, there is an urgent need to extend the coverage of the SAFTA to "substantially all trade" in the region as per the WTO requirements.

In Southeast Asia, the FTA between the members of the Association of Southeast Asian Nations (ASEAN) and the ASEAN Investment Area has helped promote intra-regional investment, and South Asia should seriously look at this model to exploit the investment-trade nexus in the region. Unlike the East Asian countries, South Asian countries have been slow in upgrading their export profile in favour of knowledge-intensive and high value-added goods that are fast moving. The production structure in South Asia is still dominated by labour-intensive, highly price-sensitive, and low value added goods such as textiles, garments, leather goods and primary products. There is a need for regional cooperation through intra-industry specialization and vertical integration that has the potential in strengthening the competitiveness in the region.

While India has emerged as a global hub for the out-sourcing of ICT services, the other South Asian countries are yet to exploit the full potential of trade in services. In this context, some of the findings of a study by the SAARC Secretariat on 'Potential for Trade in Services in the Context of SAFTA' are worth highlighting. A noteworthy finding is that the trade in services within the region was more balanced with smaller and less developed economies generally enjoying surpluses with larger economies, thus helping to bridge the asymmetries that exist in trade in goods in the region (SAARC, 2008). Autonomous liberalisation in services in the SAARC member countries has contributed to stimulating some trade in services in the region. In the case of India and Sri Lanka, deepening trade under the FTA has automatically triggered liberalisation in services which has further contributed to stimulating trade in goods.

Countries in South Asia experience high trade costs due to inadequacy in trade and transport facilitation. South Asian trade is constrained by poor infrastructure, congestion, high costs and lengthy delays. These problems are particularly severe at border crossings, many of which post significant barriers to trade. Thus, improving connectivity to facilitate trade and investment flows in the region is important. With regard to transport connectivity, a case could be made for a SAARC Regional Transport and Transit Agreement that would facilitate surface transport links throughout the region. It has been estimated that the potential transit revenue earned by Bangladesh from Indian trucks transiting through its territory to the north could be of the order of US$1 billion a year. The case could also be made to revive an Afghanistan–Pakistan–India–Bangladesh–Myanmar international corridor, which could emerge as Asia's new 'Silk Route' connecting Central Asia with East Asia, besides facilitating intra-SAARC trade, and making South Asia the hub for Pan-Asia trade. RIS (2008) recommends a South Asian Common Transport Policy to provide a comprehensive framework to facilitate regional connectivity through different modes of transport. It also recommends a South Asia Regional Infrastructure Development facility as a centre for cross-border infrastructure projects, within the ambit of the South Asia Development Fund.

The region is vulnerable owing to inadequate energy endowments and overwhelming dependence on imported fossil fuels. Regional connectivity could assist to ensure energy security. The complementary energy resource endowments in the region — Pakistan and

Bangladesh — natural gas; India — coal and petroleum products; Nepal and Bhutan — hydropower — provide a basis for regional energy cooperation. To facilitate this, the SAARC Working Group on Energy needs to be strengthened. The RIS report argues that the SAARC Energy Centre should foster collaboration with multilateral bodies, with other energy blocs, and with sources of energy technology. As energy trade requires costly infrastructure involving large investment, the report makes a case for a regional cooperative framework for facilitating trade and investment in energy. It also recommends a SAARC Energy Charter Treaty to provide a legal basis and level playing field for all members.

South Asia has emerged as one of the fastest growing regions with an average growth rate of eight per cent over the past five years. Yet, the region continues to be the home for over 40 per cent of the world's poor and fares poorly in terms of different indicators of human development, such as education, health, nutrition, and sanitation. This is worrying and the danger is that the current downside risks posed by the deterioration of the external environment could slow down South Asian growth and further aggravate poverty and human development. South Asia can face this challenge much more effectively with deeper regional economic integration.

For far too long, the economic logic of integration in South Asia has been overwhelmed by geo-political considerations, and now with the deteriorating global economic environment, renewed effort must be made to give economic integration a chance in order to realise fully South Asia's potential for rapid and inclusive growth. An integrated South Asia will be able to secure its due place in the emerging broader regional architecture in Asia and above all, exercise its role in shaping global governance.

Conclusion

Although rapid opening up took place in all South Asian countries, the reforms slowed down and in some countries slightly reversed over the years. The World Bank (2004) South Asia Trade Policy Review shows that the levels of protection increased in most South Asian countries after the initial reforms.

The latest research findings on factors explaining the overall economic growth in South Asia have come to the conclusion that capital accumulation has been the dominant factor (Ahluwalia and Williamson, 2003). Although Total Factor Productivity contribution to growth in South Asia is of minor importance (compared to capital accumulation), it was relatively higher than other developing countries, including East Asia. The contribution of human capital to growth has been modest, according to these findings.

Some have argued that, given the excessive rigidities in the South Asian economies, the slightest opening up is able to unleash tremendous growth momentum. Deverajan (2005) has, on the other hand, argued that many South Asian countries have managed to circumvent various existing controls and problems and grown. In Bangladesh for example, non-government organisations have managed to circumvent existing state controls and mushroomed, and they are playing a key role in providing a boost to overall economic activities. In Sri Lanka, for instance, nearly 90 per cent of GDP is concentrated outside the conflict zone and fairly insulated from the day-to-day events of the conflict. Thus, despite uncertainty created by the conflict for investors, somehow, existing investors have expanded and new investors have managed their way through in the system.

India's recent success story has been subjected to intense scrutiny. Panagariya (2008) argues that the economic reforms were the key to India's unprecedented growth achievements. Subramanian (2008) presents a somewhat different viewpoint where he argues that the initial investment in human resource development and skill improvement was the key to development. Whatever the case may be, the reality is that India is emerging as an economic power in the region and its neighbours should capitalise on India's strength.

India will embark on an FTA with European Union and ASEAN in 2009. It already has FTAs with many countries. It has a Comprehensive Economic Cooperation Agreement with Singapore. India can carry other South Asian countries with deeper economic integration under SAFTA, however, regional politics makes this integration slow. Three South Asian countries have FTAs with India. India has unilaterally offered duty free entry (subject to a negative list) to goods from neigbouring least developed countries. India's trade with China has grown five times during the last decade (US$40 billion). India is advocating the creation of an Asia Economic Community. As a first step, India is promoting a dialogue under an initiative known as JACIK (Japan, ASEAN, China, India and Korea). India–ASEAN FTA is seen as a first step towards a future JACIK. India's emergence as a global power is beneficial to its neighbours and South Asia's rise will be influenced by India's growth and development. There are signs that this is happening despite political obstacles in the way. However, India's influence on other South Asian nations' growth can be further strengthened by deeper economic integration in South Asia.

References

ADB (2008). *Asian Economic Outlook: 2008*, ADB, Manila.

Ahluwalia, I.J. and J. Williamson (2003). 'Introduction', in Ahulawalia, I.J. and J. Wilamson (eds.), *The South Asian Experience with Growth*, OUP, Delhi.

Chowdhury, A. and W. Mahumud (2008). *Handbook on the South Asian Economies*, Edward Elgar, United Kingdom.

Deverajan, S. (2005). 'South Asian Surprises', *Economic and Political Weekly*, Vol. XI, No. 37.

Dossani, R. (2008). *India Arriving: How this Powerhouse is Redefining Global Business*, Amcom, New York.

Hamid, N. (2007). 'South Asia: A Development Strategy for the Information Age', South Asia Department, ADB (mimeo).

Nath, K. (2007). *India's Century: The Age of Entrepreneurship in the World's Biggest Democracy*, McGraw-Hill, Delhi.

Panagariya, A. (2008). *India: The Emerging Giant*, OUP, New Delhi.

RIS (2008). *South Asia Development and Cooperation Report 2008*, prepared by Research and Information Systems (RIS), New Delhi, published by OUP, Delhi.

Subramanian, A. (2008). *India's Turn: Understanding the Economic Transformation*, OUP, New Delhi.

World Bank (2004). *Trade Policies in South Asia: An Overview* (in three volumes), Poverty Reduction and Economic Management Sector Unit, South Asia Region, The World Bank, Washington D.C.

Chapter 4

Reducing Poverty: How Much?
How Soon?

Praful Patel

Introduction

When I was asked to write a chapter on poverty in South Asia, I did not hesitate for a second. For the last five years, this topic has been at the centre of my professional life. And from the very fist day in 2003 when I was appointed as Vice President for South Asia in the World Bank, the issue of *poverty reduction, how much?, how soon?* has preoccupied me, not only within the World Bank in its efforts to help South Asian countries fight poverty but also as the question I am asked most often outside the World Bank. As can be expected, I have my own answers to this question and I would like to depart from the norm and begin this chapter with the answers and then work backward to make a few comments.

However, first I would like to make an important qualification — the global financial crisis currently unfolding will certainly have a big impact on South Asia's growth prospects going forward. The full ramifications have yet to be determined. We have already begun to see downward revisions of growth rates, for example, the World Bank has recently revised growth for developing countries to around 4.5 per cent. At the same time, we have heard more optimistic views from South Asian leaders — Prime Minister Manmohan Singh recently said that India's growth rate will continue to more or less be in line with the 11th Plan projections. My sense is that the crisis will have a negative impact and slow down growth in the immediate future.

The medium and longer term outlook will depend on several factors, including how the current crisis is resolved and how South Asian countries themselves deal with their development agendas. I believe that the past record of higher growth in the region represents a solid platform for the region to get back on a continuing high growth path in the medium to long term.

Can the Fight against Poverty in South Asia be Won? The Answer is: "Yes, but it will not be easy"

"Yes", because South Asia has been in the grips of a "growth momentum" for the past decade during which the dynamics of policy-making has changed and inspiring progress on reducing poverty has been accomplished. "Not easy" because most of the key obstacles stem from a policy or institutional failure whose reform is deeply political. And, anything political is hard to reform. We should remember that these policies and institutions were often introduced with the best of intentions, and often to protect the poor. However, in many cases, they have now become obstacles rather than enablers.

Poverty can and must be reduced. Absolute poverty, the most extreme form of deprivation, can be eliminated. The world has many examples of countries which have done this — the most recent examples being in East Asia in countries such as Malaysia, Thailand, Vietnam and China. How much and how soon? Most South Asian countries are on track to meet the poverty Millennium Development Goals (MDG) which target cutting in half the one dollar a day kind of poverty by 2015 (Figure 1). In 1990 South Asia had the second-highest proportion of people living on less than US$1 a day (43 per cent) but has made substantial progress in reducing poverty (to 30.8 per cent in 2005) and on current trends may surpass the target in 2015.[1] With sustained high growth, the trend should continue

---

[1] In this chapter poverty numbers are based on extreme poverty defined as the proportion of individuals in developing countries who live on less than US$1 a day (based on purchasing power parity 1993 constant prices). New poverty estimates published by the World Bank in 2008 reveal that 1.4 billion people in the developing

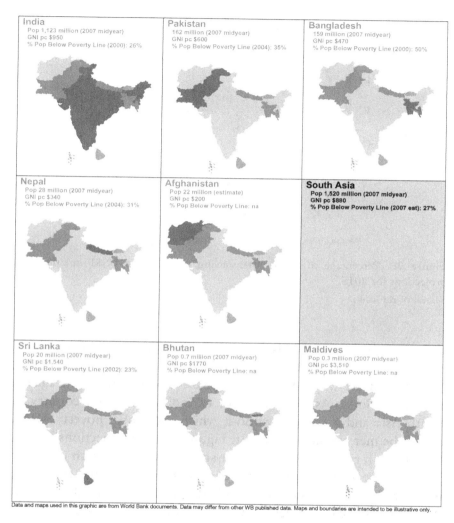

Figure 1:   Population in South Asia below poverty line

world (one in four) were living on less than US$1.25 a day in 2005, down from 1.9 billion (one in two) in 1981. In South Asia, the US$1.25 poverty rate has fallen from 60 per cent to 40 per cent over 1981–2005, but again, not enough to bring down the total number of poor people in the region, which stood at about 600 million in 2005. In India, poverty at US$1.25 a day in 2005 prices increased from 420 million people in 1981 to 455 million in 2005, while the poverty rate as a share of the total population went from 60 per cent in 1981 to 42 per cent in 2005.

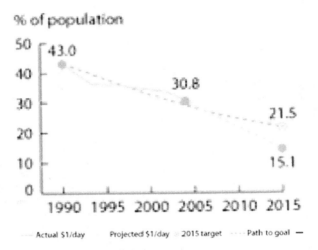

Figure 2: Percentage of South Asians living on less than US$1 in 2004 and projections for 2015.

Source: World Bank.

and in my assessment it is certainly within our reach to eliminate absolute poverty in South Asia within the next decade.

To illustrate why I believe it is possible to win the fight against poverty in South Asia, the example of India, the largest country in South Asia and a country without which the global poverty MDG cannot be met, would be relevant. Figure 3 shows projections assuming a growth rate of 10 per cent per annum. Even if growth is slowed down in the short term by the current global financial crisis, the downward poverty trend line is likely to remain in the medium term. With good policies, implementation and scaling up of ongoing programs, prospects for poverty reduction over the next decade could follow the trend lines in this graph.

I should note that while statistics are important in the tracking of progress, they can, by their very matter-of-factness, numb the harsh reality of poverty. It is not about numbers or money. Poverty is about lives on the margins of society; dependent on barely productive lands and livelihoods, people always at the tail-end of basic infrastructure,

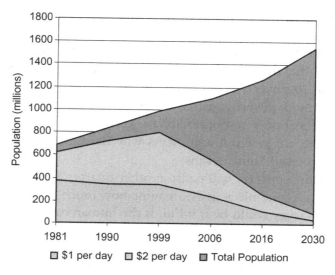

Figure 3: Dramatic reduction of poverty in India, with 10 per cent per year GDP growth

Source: World Bank.

be it drinking water, irrigation, or roads, excluded from access to basic health, education, personal security, and political representation. A single disaster — whether brought on by nature as in the recent earthquakes, tsunami, or cyclones, or man-made as we are witnessing currently in the global financial crisis — can undo hard earned progress, with devastating impact on the poor who are invisible, voiceless and powerless.

I have witnessed first hand, during many visits to villages in South Asia, what getting out of poverty means and I have seen examples of interventions that are lifting millions of poor people out of poverty. In Bangladesh I met Hena Akhtar, whose family was made homeless by the construction of Jamuna bridge. Now, with support from BRAC, she supports a family of five and sends her three children to school — a dream never realised in her own childhood. Another example is Kamalamma, whom I met during a visit to a village in Andhra Pradesh in India. She is one of the eight million women in

Andhra Pradesh who, by dint of their enterprise and energy — and the small space created by opportunity — have pulled themselves out of poverty in the last 10 years. So, I know from first hand experience that the right kind of interventions at the right scale can indeed lead to poverty reduction.

Why should poverty matter to us all? Apart from the ethical matter of a nation's responsibility to assure each citizen a life of dignity, there are practical arguments why the fight against poverty should concern all South Asians.

Eliminating poverty will enlist another quarter of the population in productive economic activity. Imagine how much more spectacular South Asia's story could be if it builds the human capital of the third of its population left outside.

Everyone talks of South Asia's 'demographic dividend'. With over half of its citizens below the age of 30, it can supply young, dynamic human resources to an ageing world. However, this dividend will be squandered unless all strata of society join to invest in the potential of South Asia's youth.

As such, eliminating poverty is not a matter of reducing to zero the number living under a dollar-a-day. Poverty's wasteland stretches far beyond, touching tens of millions of South Asians living under two-dollars-a-day and millions more under five-dollars-a-day, neither of which is anything less than degrading or deprived. Eliminating poverty requires a broad-based strategy that engages all citizens, that offers inclusion and representation along with sustainable livelihoods.

Where We Have Come From and Where We Are Now

First let us look at the current situation. The eight South Asian countries covered in this chapter are Afghanistan, Bangladesh, Bhutan, India, Maldives, Nepal, Pakistan and Sri Lanka. These countries constitute the member nations of the South Asian Association for Regional Cooperation, established in 1985 with all these nations except Afghanistan, which joined the group last year.

At the time of independence of India and Pakistan, half of South Asia's population lived below the poverty line. Today, this figure is down to under 30 per cent. Nonetheless, in absolute numbers, poverty's challenge remains daunting. About half a billion South Asians — roughly four times the population of Brazil — live in deprivation. One in every three poor persons in the world is a South Asian. One in every four Indians is poor.

Let me briefly comment where South Asia has come from and where it stands today and highlight five areas of accomplishments and future challenges in the fight against poverty:

o Recent trends in high **growth rates** which have contributed to significant poverty reduction;
o status of some **key indicators** of poverty;
o the picture with respect to growing **inequality**; and
o the importance of inclusive growth, **political economy** issues, and **crises, disasters and other shocks**.

Given their large influence on how South Asia fares in the coming decade, these represent an overall context for the last part of this chapter which will focus of what South Asia needs to do on the fight against poverty.

Recent trends of high growth rates

Compared to 3.7 per cent growth per year during 1960–80, South Asia witnessed a rapid and robust rise in its gross domestic product (GDP) growth to 5.7 per cent during 1980–2000, further accelerating towards six–nine per cent in 2006 — the highest in the last 25 years. This impressive growth rate was accompanied by significant reduction in poverty.

o India registered nine per cent growth last year and lifted 10 million people a year out of poverty. Long buried is Lal's infamous "Hindu rate of growth" that depicted India as a slow giant.
o It has been similarly heartening to see high growth in the same period in other South Asian countries — Bangladesh, Pakistan and Sri Lanka grew at nearly seven per cent a year. And Bangladesh's rate of poverty reduction is twice that of India, putting to rest Henry Kissinger's image of Bangladesh as a "basket case".

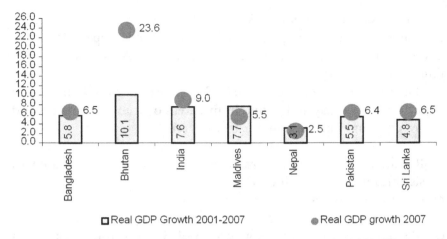

Figure 4:   GDP growth rates of South Asian countries 2001–07

Source: World Bank.

o Even Nepal, which has had anemic growth, managed to reduce
   poverty by 11 percentage points in eight years.
o However, growth has been on a declining trend since 2006. In
   2008, adjustments forced by several terms of trade shocks have
   slowed down growth. The onset of the current global financial
   crisis will further weaken South Asia's growth. The World Bank
   projections for 2009 and 2010 suggest growth rates of 6.3 per
   cent per annum for the region.

Notwithstanding the impressive economic progress, as I have noted
earlier, South Asia remains home to the world's largest concentration
of people living in extreme poverty. Thus, sustaining the highest
possible growth rates must be a top priority in South Asia.

Key Indicators

Over the past two decades, considerable progress has been accomplished in South Asia in some of the key indicators of poverty, including most of the MDGs (see South Asia MDG scorecard in Annex 1).
The good news here, as evident from the scorecard, is that South Asia

has had encouraging success in many of the MDGs. For example, mortality in children under five has reduced substantially between 1990 and 2004 (from 129 to 92 per 1,000), especially in Bangladesh (149 to 77 per 1,000), Nepal (145 to 76 per 1,000), and Sri Lanka (32 to 14 per 1,000). School enrolments at primary and secondary levels have improved.

However, there are also some other critical indicators where similar progress has not taken place. Under-5 mortality rates remain at 80 to 100 for 1,000 live births (compared to under 10 for 1,000 live births in the developed world). South Asia also has some of the worst levels of human deprivation on the planet. Pakistan, for example, has enjoyed six per cent annual GDP growth since 2002, but one in 10 children still dies before his or her fifth birthday and only 57 per cent complete primary school. India has levels of child under-nutrition nearly double those of Sub-Saharan Africa. About half of all children under the age of five are malnourished in Bangladesh and Nepal. Trends on Tuberculosis and HIV/AIDS remain problematic in the region. Without a healthy and educated workforce, South Asia will not be able to sustain current levels of economic growth. Without substantial reductions in child mortality and out-of-school children, South Asia will not end poverty.

Another issue of concern when looking at national statistics is that national averages tend to hide variations at the state or local levels, thereby neglecting to identify the critical problem of the widening gap between the 'haves' and the 'have-nots' (the "two Asias" syndrome which will be discussed in later sections). This is true not just for India with big disparities among states and regions but also for smaller countries of the region such as Nepal. Poverty assessments carried out by the Bank on most of the region's countries show stark regional and social inequalities on key poverty indicators.

Inequality, inclusive growth

In noting some of the not so good news associated with the past decade of impressive growth rates in South Asia, the issue of inequality — the fruits of this growth not reaching all citizens — deserves special emphasis

Figure 5:   Lagging regions of South Asia

Source: World Bank.
Note: The map above differentiates South Asia by per capita income comparison to national averages. Lagging regions are shaded.

as a potential threat to South Asia's future. Even as South Asia blazes a path to the world's third largest region in terms of the size of economy, its lagging regions (Figure 5) are mired in the highest levels of poverty globally. The 'Two South Asias' of the subcontinent has long been a cliché. Economists model it in their development plans; politicians exploit it in election campaigns; and travel writers weave it into brochures as the eternal enigma of South Asia. Like all clichés, however, it is very much rooted in reality.

As we look at the impressive growth performance, statistics should not neglect the trend of rising inequality taking place at the same time. South Asia is no longer one low-income region. It is a region of growing contrasts with substantial differences not only between countries, (for example, the difference between Afghanistan and Nepal and the rest of the region) but also large disparities within countries. The widening gap between the 'haves' and 'have-nots' is generating considerable social and political concern. Figure 5 depicts, in very rough terms, the two faces of South Asia — the "lagging" regions where most of the poor live and where per capita incomes are significantly below the national averages and the "leading" regions which provide most of the success stories we hear about. The richer, southern states of India are growing three per cent faster than the poorer, more populous northern states. (Bihar averaged 2.2 per cent growth between 1980 and 2004, as compared to 7.2 per cent in Karnataka.) Some human development indicators for South Asia are among the worst in developing countries. India's child malnutrition rate is double that of sub-Saharan Africa. Parts of India, Sri Lanka, Bhutan and Maldives are showing clear signs of reaching middle-income status. However, Sri Lanka also has its own disparities — between the region around Colombo and the rest. Even in some of the more prosperous regions, there are dark pockets of deprivation: Maharashtra, where Mumbai paces itself against Shanghai, contains 10 of India's 100 poorest districts and has among the highest rates of farmer suicides. Bangladesh, Nepal, most of Pakistan remain low-income. Unless growth is widely shared South Asia risks widening the fault line between the 'haves' and 'have-nots'. Excluding large parts of the population from the benefits of growth (denying them the chance to get out of poverty) will only exacerbate existing socio-regional-ethnic differences and sparking fresh ones. Therefore, making growth inclusive must be a key priority going forward.

Politics and conflict

The political situation in South Asia has also been evolving, with mixed results. Nepal, Maldives and Bhutan have undergone inspiring transitions, showing early signs of more democratic governments and stability to allow greater space for development. Nepal's new Maoist-led government is making steady progress on building upon the successful process of elections for a Constituent Assembly. The elections in Pakistan were accomplished relatively smoothly, bringing an end to nearly 10-years of military rule but the country continues to face a difficult task of transitioning towards an effective government. In Bangladesh, the parliamentary elections in December 2007, after nearly two years of caretaker government appear to be set on track for returning that country to democracy. Afghanistan and Sri Lanka continue to face a very difficult security situation. And India is gearing up for general elections next year. As we know, the political economy represents perhaps the most critical factor for progress on growth, development and poverty reduction. Hopefully, the period ahead will usher in the right kind of environment — in terms of stability and security — for growth and development to continue and scale up.

A major and often talked about issue in the political economy is corruption. I will not go into detail on this subject; only mention it as an issue which looms large in South Asia, exacting a high price on development. Several South Asian countries suffer from weak governance and endemic corruption.

Another critical issue I will also simply mention here is conflict. The region has the world's largest conflict affected population — about 71 million people. Full blown conflicts in Afghanistan and Sri Lanka and simmering ones in parts of India (for example, northeast states) and Pakistan (for example, Balochistan, Afghan border areas) pose serious threats not only in terms of undoing past gains but also as serious obstacles to development.

Shocks, crises and disasters

In the last five years, price increases of global commodities, especially those of oil, metal, and food, took a toll on South Asia. Budget deficits widened and trade balances worsened. With this, the growth weakened and inflation reached double digits. Before the region could recover from the adverse impact of high commodity prices, the global financial crisis has come knocking. The cascading effects of these crises will present daunting policy challenges to South Asia.

The region has also endured, in the past five years, a number of major natural disasters such as the Tsunami in India, Sri Lanka and Maldives, the earthquake in Pakistan, and floods and cyclones in Bangladesh and India. These disasters have exacted a huge price not only setting back development progress but also directly impacting the poor, bringing back millions of people back into poverty. South Asia will continue to be vulnerable to natural disasters. It is a region trapped between the melting snows of the Himalayas and the rising waters of the oceans. Four hundred million people — if it were a country, it would be the third largest in the world — rely on the Ganges river and its tributaries for their livelihood. Six thousand rivers provide a perennial source of irrigation and power to one of the world's most densely populated and poorest areas. However, alongside the potential benefits to the populations of Bangladesh, India and Nepal, there is also the continuing threat that climate change poses to poor and already vulnerable people of these countries.

The combination of impressive accomplishments and huge challenges described above is the context facing South Asia as it ends its first decade of rapid growth and contemplates the next decade of fast growth. In the final part of this chapter, I shall briefly outline what it will take for South Asia to win the fight against poverty.

The Challenge Ahead: What Must South Asia do to Eliminate Poverty? What will it Take? Can South Asia do it?

What will it take to end poverty in South Asia? South Asia is at a crossroads. A second decade of rapid growth is not guaranteed. South Asians can be complacent with lower growth and make slow progress on inequality, human development, and weak governance. Or they can leverage their recent high growth achievement, build on success and end mass poverty in a generation. Hence, the challenge is obvious — how to build upon and extend the unprecedented economic progress in the region, and to bring more of the potential benefits to the hundreds of millions still trapped in poverty.

To my mind there are three key prerequistes which should be given priority by every country in South Asia:

  i) Returning to sustained higher growth track;
 ii) Faster progress on human development; and
iii) Making development inclusive.

I will briefly comment on each.

Returning to sustained higher growth track. To repeat what I have already said, South Asian countries will need to accelerate and sustain their economic growth rates. If they can maintain high growth rates — before the current crisis I used to say eight per cent a year, and would stick with that figure as a medium term target to achieve in the period leading to 2015 — income poverty in the subcontinent could fall to single-digits in two decades. As I have already said, this will not be easy. For one thing, South Asia faces severe infrastructure constraints — power cuts, blocked ports, congested roads, inefficient railways are all part of the landscape. These will make it difficult to even maintain current growth rates. Services-led growth that bypasses this infrastructure will also bypass labor-intensive manufacturing growth needed for creating millions of new jobs. For another, savings and investment rates in South Asia are much lower than those in East Asia — the only other region to achieve such high growth rates in recent times.

o *Infrastructure Deficit.* South Asia faces formidable infrastructure deficits. Power outages and load shedding are common. Not a single city in South Asia is able to deliver drinking water 24 hours, seven days a week even though, in most cases, there is plenty of water available. Traffic congestion is bringing many a city in South Asia to a standstill. Among the reasons for these deficits is the lack of investment in the past, under-spending on operations and maintenance, weak regulation. I think there was also possibly an optimistic view — for which donors must accept the lion's share of the blame — that the private sector will "take care" of infrastructure.

○ But these are only proximate reasons for the deficits; at the heart of the problem is how infrastructure is managed. For example, most utilities in South Asia are run directly by political leaders. The Chairperson of Water Boards in India, for example, in many cases, is the Chief Minister of the state. There is little distance between the policy maker and service provider — judge and jury are one and the same. Under these conditions, political considerations, not service delivery objectives, drive the provision of services. The pricing of infrastructure services reflects these political decisions. Prices of electricity and water have been kept deliberately low so that poor people can afford them. However, the outcome has been everything but a decrepit electricity grid, intermittent service and deficit-ridden utilities. The Ceylon Electricity Board, for example, loses 50 million rupees every day. That is the cost of one rural hospital. Worse, poor people, the very ones for whom the prices were kept low, are usually left out of the electricity or water networks. They end up buying it in the private market at about five to sixteen times the metre rate. Various estimates suggest that India needs to invest about eight per cent of GDP mainly in water and power infrastructure to sustain growth. Much of the needed investment can be financed by better pricing of infrastructure.

○ *This is no secret.* So why have South-Asian governments not been more pro-active in changing how infrastructure is managed? Simply put, this a deeply political act, not simply a question of applying technocratic solutions.

○ *Subsidised electricity is a good example.* There are winners and losers. The winners can mobilise themselves to block the reform. One of the most distorting and inequitable policies is the practice in some Indian states of giving free power to farmers. Yet, when Chandra Babu Naidu, the Chief Minister of Andhra Pradesh, reformed the policy, he lost the election. His opponent ran on the platform that, if elected, he would restore free power, which he did. I have to admit that the World Bank has not always helped. Given the enormous distortions and losses of the utilities, the World Bank, in the past, took a rather absolutist position, saying that we would not lend for infrastructure unless there was reform. As a result, there was neither reform nor infrastructure investment. Over time, we have realised that this is not productive. In the past three years, we have been working with governments, using a mix of financial and knowledge assistance, to help them reform and crowd-in investments in infrastructure.

Faster progress on human development. Human development is lagging behind economic growth in most South Asian countries. Investing in people with effective programmes has to be a central priority with special attention to learning from experience of failed programs.

o One glaring example of failure is the high rates of absenteeism among teachers in public schools and doctors in primary health clinics. In India, the average rates are 25 and 40 per cent respectively. Even when providers are present, the quality of services provided is appallingly low. As a result, 80 per cent of health spending is in the private sector. Poor people bypass the free, public clinic and pay the private doctor (who may be a quack) because, at least, he is present and treats them well.

o The problem is the failure of service providers to be accountable either to policymakers or to their clients. Public-school teachers are absent because no one is monitoring them; and they collect their paycheck even if they do not show up for work. Changing this situation is changing the politics of the sector — again a task beyond the traditional technocratic solutions.

Therefore, what can be done? One path is to change the incentives is to make schools and health care providers more accountable for performance.

o In Bangladesh, they do this by giving students — in this case, female secondary school students — a choice. Girls can chose between public, private, non-government organisation-run, or madrassa and the schools are compensated according to the number of girls they enroll. Not only is secondary school enrolment rising rapidly in

Bangladesh — and twice as fast for girls as for boys — but many schools now have separate latrines for girls and boys. Schools are hiring female teachers to attract more girls to enroll there.

o A second way to make schools accountable is to have parents and the local community participate in their management. Nepal has handed of the running of 5,000 public schools to management committees consisting of parents, teachers and respected members of the local community. Teacher and student absenteeism is down, and the programme is likely to cover all schools in the country before long.

o A third form of strengthening accountability is to allow schools to hire teachers from the local community, as is being done in Punjab, Pakistan. While they may be less qualified than the public sector teachers, these people are more reliable in attendance. Also, some studies show that the quality of teaching is not significantly different from that by more qualified (and more expensive) teachers from urban areas.

o Finally, contracting out health services increases accountability and appears to improve outcomes. In Afghanistan, an independent evaluation of a programme of contracting out health services showed, among other things, that about 40,000 babies a year were saved from dying before their first birthday, a tremendous turnaround in a country which had among the highest infant mortality rates in the world.

Making development more inclusive. To summarise, South Asia will need to reverse the trend of rising inequality. Inequality is rising in South Asia partly because certain well-intentioned policies have backfired, making it harder for poor people to benefit from growth. Ensuring growth benefits all should therefore be another key goal for all South Asian countries.

o In Sri Lanka, for example, agricultural policies have fueled inequality. Economic growth has been concentrated in the western province. The rest of the country has not grown because agriculture has hardly expanded, in large part due to policies that restrict farmers to growing rice rather than allowing them to diversify their crops. Recently, a farmer was fined 35,000 rupees for growing bananas on his land. However, even though the evidence is clear that changing the rice policy would enhance growth and benefit the poor, political inertia makes this a difficult shift.

o Another source of rising inequality in South Asia is the lack of unskilled employment growth. In India, Pakistan and Sri Lanka especially, economic growth has not been accompanied by a commensurate increase in employment. A major reason for this is the set of restrictive labor regulations in most of these countries. The average severance pay in Sri Lanka is 175 weeks. Not surprisingly, firms stay out of the formal sector so they can avoid these regulations. In Sri Lanka, the number of employees per firm peaks at 14. Why? Because the employment regulations kick in at 15 workers. However, informal sector firms cannot invest in large-scale equipment that will then give employment to significant numbers of workers. In short, due to some restrictive employment regulations, low-skilled manufacturing employment has not grown in South Asia. The solution is not to get rid of these restrictions, but to replace them with regulations that provide workers with adequate security and employers with flexibility to hire more workers. Needless to say, reforming labour laws can be political dynamite.

Economic growth is also contributing to more inclusive policies. South Asia has a sorry history of redistributive programmes that have been poorly targeted, and frequently used as tools of political patronage. Sri Lanka's cash transfer program, Samurdhi, excluded 40 per cent of the poor, while 44 per cent of its beneficiaries were not poor. Increasing inequality has created pressure to reform these programmes, and politicians are responding. Samurdhi is being revamped. South Asia can build on successful indigenous examples of development innovations like the women's self-help groups in Andhra Pradesh which can be scaled up to good effect. India is implementing a massive programme that guarantees 100 days of work to any rural household that needs it. And safety net programmes are now receiving the attention they deserve — there is plenty of evidence that well-designed, well-targeted safety net programmes offer some of the most effective interventions reaching the poor.

Any one of the challenges I have mentioned above is daunting enough. And I have not mentioned governance which is a cross-cutting theme — a conducive environment of good governance and effective anticorruption measures is essential in supporting the three challenges. Yet, South Asian countries can — and should — overcome all three by leveraging their recent growth. Whether policy makers are able to resolve these challenges will make the difference between just advancing poverty reduction and achieving the dream of a sub-continent free of poverty within a generation.

Conclusion

I am optimistic that, in South Asia, we can end poverty in a generation. South Asia has already shown that it can accelerate growth and reduce poverty. The remaining obstacles to ending poverty — inequality, infrastructure, lagging human development, weak governance — are man-made. If we erected them, surely we can also dismantle them and enable millions more of South Asians like Hena Akhtar and Kamlamma to rise out of poverty.

Annex 1: South Asia Scorecard on MDGs

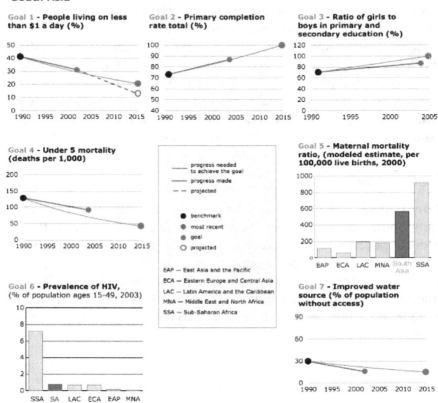

Source: World Bank.

Chapter 5

Managing Inflation: Key to South Asia's Economic Progress

Salehuddin Ahmed

Introduction

Inflation has become a major concern worldwide in recent years, and the South Asian countries are of no exception. A high rate of inflation is detrimental to sustained growth. Moreover, it adversely affects the financial sector development. Another major concern for South Asia, which is a home to the vast majority of the world's poor, is the adverse impact of inflation on the poor and other vulnerable groups in the society. Since the consumption pattern of the poor is different from that of the non-poor and the poor spend a higher share of their budget on food and other essential commodities, inflation especially fuelled by rising prices of food and other necessities hurt the poor more than the non-poor.

The main objective of macroeconomic policies in South Asian countries is to ensure economic stability together with low inflation and sustain high economic growth. As elsewhere in the world, the central banks of the South Asian countries are committed to maintaining reasonable price stability. Price stability is desirable because a rising price level (inflation) produces uncertainty hampering smooth economic growth. Although considerable debate exists regarding the nature of growth-inflation trade-off especially in low income countries, macroeconomic stability is an important pre-requisite to harness

---

The views expressed here are the author's own and do not reflect the views of the Bangladesh Bank.

rapid growth and ensure social equity in South Asia. Inflation can be costly for the poor since their purchasing power is eroded; their assets are devalued more as they hold a larger share of their assets in liquid form compared with the non-poor; and it is difficult for the poor to hedge against inflation due to their limited access to the financial system.

This chapter examines the current trends of inflation and growth in South Asian countries and suggests policy options to manage inflation at reasonable level. It is structured as follows. The second section examines recent inflation and growth situation in South Asian countries. This is followed by a more detailed analysis of Bangladesh's inflation as a case study in third section. The fourth section highlights the ways and means to manage inflation while the fifth section provides some policy options.

Growth and Inflation in South Asia

According to recent projections, growth in South Asia is likely to decelerate from 8.6 per cent in 2007 to 7.1 per cent in 2008 and to 6.7 per cent in 2009 (Table 1).[1] On the other hand, inflation is

Table 1:   Real GDP growth (per cent) in South Asian countries

Year	2005	2006	2007	2008		2009	
Countries				Base	Update	Base	Update
Afghanistan	16.1	8.2	11.5	9.0	7.5	9.0	8.3
Bangladesh	6.0	6.6	6.4	6.0	6.2	6.5	6.5
Bhutan	6.9	7.8	17.0	14.4	14.4	7.2	7.2
India	9.4	9.6	9.0	8.0	7.4	8.5	7.0
Maldives	−4.6	18.0	7.6	8.0	6.5	7.0	7.0
Nepal	2.9	4.1	2.6	3.8	5.6	4.3	5.0
Pakistan	9.0	5.8	6.8	6.3	5.8	6.5	4.5
Sri Lanka	6.2	7.7	6.8	6.0	6.0	6.0	6.0

Source: *Asian Development Outlook*, April 2008 Update, Asian Development Bank.

---

[1] *Asian Development Outlook*, April 2008 Update, Asian Development Bank.

projected to be more than double from 5.5 per cent to 11.8 per cent between 2007 and 2008, and recede to 9.2 per cent in 2009. Current account deficits are also projected to widen significantly.

In the context of the present global financial crisis, the aforementioned growth projections may be modified downwards for some countries. Even then, the point to be noted here is that some of the countries will achieve growth above the regional and global trends.

In most South Asian countries, overheating from excessive aggregate demand, aggravated by imported cost-push factors, has made inflation a critical issue calling for strengthened macro management and a sober assessment of macroeconomic priorities for designing the reform agenda for the short and medium terms. Overall, the region's growth prospects remain fundamentally strong. One reason for this is that, since the end of the Asian crisis, priority in South Asia has been to boost economic growth. In this context, a relatively loose monetary policy fueled the backward-looking inflation expectations that emerged as an important source of South Asian inflation. On the other hand, monetary policy accommodative of food and oil price shocks gave rise to forward-looking inflation expectations, somewhat reinforcing the already high backward-looking inflation expectations. This unwelcome prospects gave the region's central banks enough reasons to realise the importance of subduing inflation before it becomes entrenched and inflicts further damages to their economies. This shows the need for these economies to undergo painful trade-offs along with much needed corrective policy measures.

In reality, the present growth–inflation tradeoff facing the South Asian countries appears favourable mainly because the growth prospect of the region remains fundamentally robust. Although the loss of output due to anti-inflationary tightening policies could somewhat dent the region's growth, it is unlikely to push the region into recession. However, it would still take a great deal of political courage to decisively act in controlling inflationary forces.

As with many other developing countries, surging inflation, deteriorating current account balances, worsening fiscal balances and depreciating local currencies have hit South Asian countries in varying degrees during the current inflation episode. In South Asia, inflation

Table 2:   Inflation rate (per cent) in South Asian countries

Year	2005	2006	2007	2008		2009	
Countries				Base	Update	Base	Update
Afghanistan	12.3	5.1	13.0	10.2	24.0	7.2	9.5
Bangladesh	6.5	7.2	7.2	9.0	9.9	8.0	9.0
Bhutan	4.8	4.9	5.2	4.5	10.0	4.5	7.0
India	4.4	5.4	4.7	4.5	11.5	5.0	7.5
Maldives	3.3	3.5	7.4	6.0	11.0	6.0	6.0
Nepal	4.5	8.0	6.4	7.0	7.9	6.5	8.5
Pakistan	9.3	7.9	7.8	8.0	12.0	6.5	20.0
Sri Lanka	11.0	10.0	15.8	16.2	24.0	14.0	18.0

Source: Asian Development Outlook, April 2008 Update, Asian Development Bank.

accelerated in 2008 reaching double digits by mid-2008 in most countries (Table 2). In particular, food price inflation emerged as the major concern since food consumption covers a high proportion of consumer spending, especially for the poor. In addition, the countries were adversely affected by adjustments in administrated fuel prices through, for example, higher costs of transportation and for operating farm equipment in the backdrop of rising and volatile oil prices in the world market. The weakening of local currencies against the United States dollar especially in India and Pakistan in 2008 also contributed to inflation pressures, exacerbating the rise in global commodity and import prices.

The impact on the current account was, however, partly relieved by a strong performance in services exports (India and Maldives) and robust workers' remittances (Bangladesh, Nepal and Sri Lanka). Slowdown or reversal of capital inflows in the wake of current economic problems in some South Asian countries also emerged as an area of concern. Moreover, elections expected in 2008 and 2009 in several South Asian countries (for example, Bangladesh and India) may delay further price adjustments and subsidy cut, leading to worsened fiscal balances. Similarly, tighter credit conditions and higher interest rates in several South Asian countries may dampen investment, with slower economic growth.

Table 3: Current account balance (per cent of GDP) in South Asian countries

Year	2005	2006	2007	2008		2009	
Countries				Base	Update	Base	Update
Afghanistan	−2.8	−4.9	0.9	0.5	0.6	−1.2	−3.1
Bangladesh	−0.9	1.3	1.4	0.7	0.9	1.0	0.5
Bhutan	−30.4	−4.3	10.5	10.1	10.1	2.4	2.4
India	−1.2	−1.1	−1.5	−2.2	−3.1	−2.6	−3.6
Maldives	−36.4	−33.0	−40.1	−45.0	−50.9	−40.0	−40.0
Nepal	2.0	2.2	−0.1	1.0	1.9	1.0	1.5
Pakistan	−1.6	−3.9	−4.8	−6.3	−8.4	−5.8	−8.0
Sri Lanka	−2.7	−5.3	−4.2	−4.3	−8.2	−4.2	−8.4

Source: *Asian Development Outlook*, April 2008 Update, Asian Development Bank.

Country-Specific Developments

Afghanistan has been facing a strong challenge in managing both inflation and growth. The current account balance showed a mixed trend over the years and is projected to deteriorate in 2009. The inflation rate is estimated at 24 per cent in 2008, compared with 13 per cent in 2007. This is mainly due to poor harvest, high food and fuel prices, and fragile law and order situation hampering movement of goods within the country. The growth of gross domestic product (GDP) has been estimated lower at 7.5 per cent in 2008 from 11.5 per cent in 2007.

Bangladesh achieved a growth rate of 6.2 per cent and a current account surplus of 0.9 per cent of the GDP in FY2008. The economy showed significant resilience in recovering from recurrent floods followed by a cyclone (Sidr) during the year. The average consumer price index (CPI) inflation moved up to ten per cent in June 2008 mainly fed by supply-side factors dominated by high commodity prices in the international market and a shortfall in domestic food grain production due to natural calamities. In response, among other measures, the government reduced import duties on food grains and other essential food items, introduced subsidised sales of food grains for the poor and lowered interest rate on import credit in order to boost import of essential commodities. The Bangladesh Bank, the

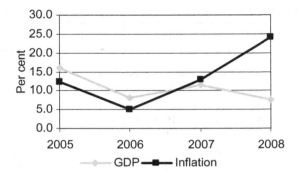

Figure 1:   GDP growth rate and inflation rate of Afghanistan
Source: Asian Development Outlook, April 2008 Update, Asian Development Bank.

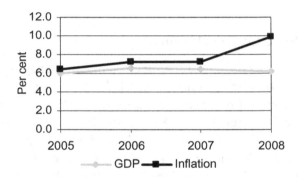

Figure 2:   GDP growth rate and inflation rate of Bangladesh
Source: Asian Development Outlook, April 2008 Update, Asian Development Bank.

country's central bank, pursued growth supportive monetary policy stance permitting adequate flow of credit to agriculture, small and medium enterprises (SMEs), rural nonfarm sector, and other productive activities. Private sector credit also expanded in other supportive areas such as transport and communications and working capital. For keeping demand-side pressures under control, the Bangladesh Bank relied on open market operations keeping reserve requirements, the liquidity ratio and the main policy rate (reverse repurchase) unchanged for quite a while. The reverse repo rate has been increased recently by 25 basis points to 8.75.

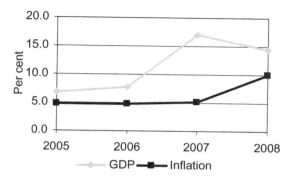

Figure 3: GDP growth rate and inflation rate of Bhutan
Source: Asian Development Outlook, April 2008 Update, Asian Development Bank.

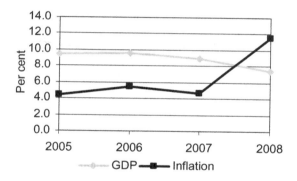

Figure 4: GDP growth rate and inflation rate of India
Source: Asian Development Outlook, April 2008 Update, Asian Development Bank.

In Bhutan, the GDP growth rate rose to 17 per cent in 2007, pulled up largely by the start up of 1,020-megawatt Tala hydropower plant in end June 2007. Given the parity peg between the currencies of Bhutan and India, price movements of the two countries were similar and in view of the price developments in India, Bhutan's projected inflation was revised upward to ten per cent in FY08.

Recent developments have given rise to significant challenges to India's strong growth performance in recent years. Emerging capacity constraints, continued rapid expansion in credit and partial

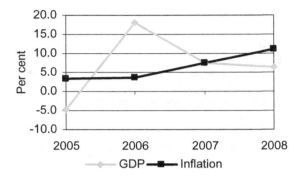

Figure 5:   GDP growth rate and inflation rate of Maldives

Source: Asian Development Outlook, April 2008 Update, Asian Development Bank.

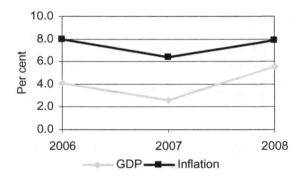

Figure 6:   GDP growth rate and inflation rate of Nepal

Source: Asian Development Outlook, April 2008 Update, Asian Development Bank.

pass-through of global commodity price increases have triggered steep domestic inflation and consequently resulted in monetary tightening. The GDP growth, which was nine per cent in 2007, was expected to decline to 7.4 per cent in 2008 and a similar growth is likely to continue in 2009 as well. The inflation rate was estimated to have risen to 11.5 per cent in 2008 from 4.7 per cent in 2007. A widening trade deficit, moderating capital inflows and some depreciation of the Rupee also feature under current developments. The main problem, however, stems from large fiscal imbalances

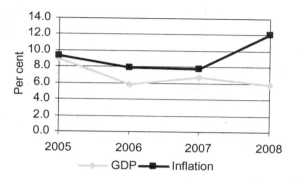

Figure 7:   GDP growth rate and inflation rate of Pakistan

Source: *Asian Development Outlook*, April 2008 Update, Asian Development Bank.

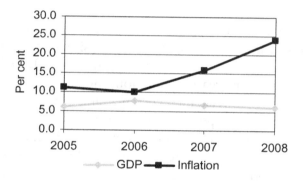

Figure 8:   GDP growth rate and inflation rate of Sri Lanka

Source: *Asian Development Outlook*, April 2008 Update, Asian Development Bank.

created by escalating oil and other subsidies, and other unbudgeted liabilities. The key to ensuring macroeconomic stability and unleashing the country's enormous growth potential lies on how well the government addresses the difficult budgetary issues in order to maintain macroeconomic stability and implement long-term structural reforms.

Economic growth in Maldives was estimated at 6.5 per cent in 2008. The consumer price index, reflecting the escalating costs of food and fuel, moved up to 15.5 per cent (year-on-year) in June 2008, raising the average inflation for the year to 11 per cent. Resulting mainly from expansionary fiscal policy, high import dependency, and rising fuel and food prices, the current account deficit widened to more than 40 per cent of the GDP in 2007. These impacts seem to have strengthened in 2008 resulting the projected current account deficit to deteriorate to nearly 51 per cent of the GDP.

The recent political developments in Nepal offer grounds for cautious hope. The GDP growth rebounded to 5.6 per cent in 2008 from 2.6 per cent in 2007, supported by weather-induced recovery in agriculture. The growth revival was also aided by the continued expansion of services activities. As a result of sharp increases in food and oil prices, the year-on-year inflation rose to 7.9 per cent in 2008.

However, higher remittances and tourism receipts helped to more than offset the widening trade deficit to result in a current account surplus of 1.9 per cent of the GDP (compared with a deficit of 0.1 per cent in the previous year).

The surge in global oil and food prices and domestic policy uncertainties within a turbulent political situation created heavy stress on the Pakistan economy in 2008. This was reflected in a slow-down in growth an increase in inflation, much larger fiscal and current account deficits, weakening currency, and a large drop in foreign reserves. Increased risk perception was seen in the downgrading of credit ratings, rise in sovereign bond spreads, slide in capital inflows, and declining access to international capital. With continued high oil prices, ongoing power shortages and tightened demand management policies to correct macroeconomic imbalances, economic growth was 5.8 per cent in 2008. High inflation averaged 12 per cent in 2008 as domestic fuel, food, and power subsidies were rationalized which is expected to rise further to 20 per cent in 2009 from 7.8 per cent in 2007.

Sri Lanka's economy grew by 6.8 per cent in 2007. Growth was slightly lower at around six per cent in 2008 and in 2009, mainly due to the global slowdown affecting Sri Lanka's key export markets. Point-to-point inflation hit 15.8 per cent in December 2007, driven mainly by food prices. In 2008, the government increased fuel prices several times to allow the pass-through of international oil price increases. Electricity tariffs were also revised in 2008, reflecting cost pressures on thermal power generation. This rise in administered prices contributed to pushing up inflation further reaching 28.2 per cent by end June 2008. Sri Lanka's balance of payments also remained under pressure, largely due to high global oil prices. The current account deficit markedly widened and rose to 8.2 per cent of GDP in 2008.

Responses to rising inflation have varied across countries in South Asia. Some countries (for example, India) tightened monetary policy by hiking interest rates and tightening reserve requirements. India also intervened in the foreign exchange market to support its currency. On the other hand, the fiscal policy stance was eased in many countries, reflecting significant increases in food and fuel subsidies. This suggests that the economic cycle in South Asia started to turn especially since early 2008 and more weakness is expected ahead in response to slowing demand from developed country markets and growing stress in the financial markets. In the major South Asian economies, there are already signs of slowing growth in the wake of weakening investments while private consumption and export growth need to be kept in view. The currencies have come under pressure, prompting central banks to intervene (India and Pakistan). In several countries (for example, India), underlying inflation pressures have increased as high resource utilisation and robust credit growth have created favourable grounds for second round effects in the absence of sufficient policy tightening. A major policy dilemma that the South Asian countries face at present is how to respond to the weakening growth outlook and global financial turbulence without losing sight of inflation risks that have deepened over the year. Overall, although there is considerable country divergences, downside risks to growth have risen while inflation risks have moderated in recent months as global food and fuel prices have declined. Accordingly, the South Asian countries need to adjust their policy priorities, keeping in view notable differences in country circumstances.

Inflation in Bangladesh: Key Features and Policy Responses

Keeping inflation at a reasonably low and stable level is one of the main objectives of monetary policy in Bangladesh. In view of the prominence of supply side factors in present inflation dynamics, the Bangladesh Bank has been pursuing a growth-supportive and prudent monetary policy stance to contain the uptrend in inflation and provide support to output growth.

The Bangladesh economy witnessed continued upward inflationary pressures in FY2008. The persistent rise in inflation during FY2008 was attributed to the unprecedented rise in commodity prices in the international market particularly that of food grains and fuel, shortfall in domestic food production and supply disruptions, mainly due to devastating floods and cyclone, cost escalation of domestically produced goods resulting from an increase in prices of imported inputs, and market imperfections as well as disruptions in supply chains. While the 12-month point-to-point CPI inflation showed an increase from 9.2 per cent in FY07 to 10.0 per cent in FY08, the 12-month average inflation rose from 7.2 per cent in FY07 to 9.9 per cent in FY08.

The historical trend shows that inflation in Bangladesh varies directly with food prices (Figure 9). Higher food inflation fuels overall inflation since the weightage attached to food items constitute nearly 59 per cent of the CPI. As the current inflation is dominated by soaring food prices, food inflation has been higher than non-food inflation. While the average food inflation was 1.4 per cent, compared

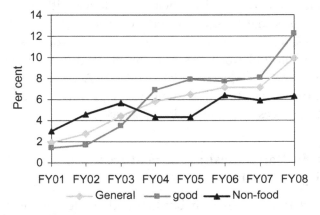

Figure 9:   Trends in national inflation rate

with the nonfood inflation rate of three per cent in FY2001, food inflation reached 12.3 per cent in FY2008, widening the gap from the nonfood inflation rate of 6.3 per cent. The gap between the 12-month average food and non-food inflation further expanded in July 2008, as food inflation rose to 12.5 per cent and non-food inflation declined slightly to 6.1 per cent. In FY2008, point-to-point food inflation showed mixed trends, while non-food inflation mostly declined. Food inflation rose from 9.8 per cent in June 2007 to 14.5 per cent in December 2007 thereafter declining to 9.6 per cent in May 2008 with frequent fluctuations. The rate of food inflation increased to 14.1 per cent at the end of June 2008. Non-food inflation, on the other hand, declined from 8.3 per cent in June 2007 to 3.5 per cent in June 2008 (Table 4).

In Bangladesh, inflation is measured separately for rural and urban areas. The expectation is that food inflation will be lower in rural areas than in urban areas while the situation will be reverse in the case of non-food inflation. During FY2001, average food inflation was 1.2 per cent in rural areas and 1.9 per cent in urban areas; while, in the case of non-food inflation, the rates were 3.8 per cent in rural areas and

Table 4: Trend of average inflation (per cent) in Bangladesh

Year	National			Rural			Urban		
	General	Food	Non-food	General	Food	Non-food	General	Food	Non-food
FY01	1.94	1.38	3.04	2.26	1.18	3.83	1.52	1.89	1.13
FY02	2.79	1.63	4.61	2.43	1.44	4.57	3.36	2.09	4.70
FY03	4.38	3.46	5.66	4.74	4.05	5.91	3.52	2.09	5.00
FY04	5.83	6.93	4.37	5.77	6.55	4.47	5.99	7.80	4.14
FY05	6.49	7.90	4.33	6.62	7.99	4.27	6.14	7.71	4.49
FY06	7.16	7.76	6.40	7.36	7.62	6.90	6.68	8.09	5.14
FY07	7.2	8.11	5.9	7.28	7.93	6.10	7.02	8.53	5.34
FY08	9.94	12.28	6.32	9.99	11.95	6.41	9.80	13.07	6.06
July 2008	10.00	12.50	6.13	10.09	12.20	6.23	9.79	13.21	5.84
August 2008	10.01	12.56	6.01	10.13	12.30	6.13	9.70	13.16	5.68

Source: Bangladesh Bureau of Statistics.

1.1 per cent in urban areas. In July 2008, average food inflation was 12.2 per cent in rural areas, compared to 13.2 per cent in urban areas. In the case of non-food category, rural areas experienced an inflation rate of 6.2 per cent in the same month while the rate was 5.8 per cent in urban areas. This shows that, in general, the urban people face a higher rate of food inflation relative to the rural population, while the rural people experience a higher rate of nonfood inflation relative to their urban counterparts.

The monetary policy of the Bangladesh Bank emphasises the need to accelerate economic growth and ensure reasonable price stability to take forward the country's poverty reduction agenda. For the purpose, the thrust is to ensure healthy macroeconomic fundamentals essential to sustaining high economic growth, shielding the economy from internal and external shocks (global price fluctuations and financial turbulences), and tapping new frontiers of development. The policy also intends to anchor inflation expectations on a realistic assessment of growth and price developments.

For achieving the objectives, the Bangladesh Bank uses monetary instruments in a prudent manner to achieve targeted real sector growth and ensure a reasonable rate of inflation. More specifically, the Bangladesh Bank routinely uses repo, reverse repo, and the Bangladesh Bank bill rates as policy instruments to influence financial and real sector prices while cash reserve requirement and statutory liquidity ratio for banks remain as sparsely used instruments to influence the volume of credit as and when needed. On the other hand, the annual monetary programme uses reserve money (RM) as the operating target and broad money as the intermediate target.

Moreover, it is now increasingly realised that the challenges facing the domestic economy in the present uncertain global economic environment require the Bangladesh Bank's monetary policy to play a key role in striking a balance between growth and price stability. This is critical for Bangladesh especially in countering any threat to macroeconomic stability and achieving poverty reduction goals. While monetary tightening can bring down inflation, it has unacceptably high cost in terms of foregone output and employment which Bangladesh can ill afford in view of its growth and poverty reduction imperatives. This, however, does not negate the importance of avoiding excessive monetary laxity which harms macro-economic stability and hence the growth and poverty reduction efforts.

In view of the aforementioned imperatives, the Bangladesh Bank's recent priority has been to pursue prudent policies that are supportive of supply-side and growth-promoting measures especially to ensure the smooth flow of credit to the economy's productive sectors especially agriculture, SMEs, and the rural economy. The policies also encourage increased flow of credit to women entrepreneurs. In order to avoid the build-up of excessive demand pressure, special attention has been given to channeling credit to its intended productive and supply augmenting uses alongside discouraging credit flows to unproductive and speculative uses. Also, in addition to refinance support for agriculture, SMEs and housing loans, new refinancing lines for socially desirable and emerging activities are under consideration by the Bangladesh Bank.

In the foreign exchange market, exchange rate stability, achieved by arresting any undue volatility, is needed to facilitate the import of essential commodities and control imported inflation. Moreover, the Bangladesh Bank's efforts have been directed to enhance the inflow of workers' remittances and increasingly divert remittance receipts to investments in productive sectors for easing potential demand pressure and expanding the economy's productive capacity. Recently, the Bangladesh Bank has made available forward hedging mechanism to importers for ensuring more efficient import of essential goods.

Obviously, the success of anti-inflation policies requires greater fiscal and monetary coordination to ensure a clear recognition of the importance of the monetary policy and to support appropriate alignment of relevant policy parameters within the overall macroeconomic framework. Maintaining fiscal discipline by the government and minimizing the dependence on financing fiscal deficit from the banking system, especially from the Bangladesh Bank, generates less inflationary pressure. It is, therefore, important to increasingly generate more revenue earnings and find alternate sources of financing such as developing an active secondary market for government securities that would contribute toward improving the quality of the Bangladesh Bank's monetary management. It is important to adopt appropriate changes in the government's debt management strategy to improve the balance between short- (for exmaple, treasury bills) and long-term borrowing (for example, through issuing bonds) since any shift in the borrowing pattern affects the conduct of the monetary policy.

Moreover, the issue of the reduction of the government's dependence on bank borrowing to finance fiscal deficits needs careful consideration for which, like in other countries, fiscal responsibility laws can be enacted to restrict government borrowing from the Bangladesh Bank and limit the government's option of having large debts. Along with promoting government savings instruments, especially targeted toward non-resident Bangladeshis, adopting fiscal responsibility and debt limitation law by the government to restrict the extent of debt monetisation would enhance the effectiveness of monetary policy instruments. In addition, the further strengthening of debt market infrastructure to promote a vibrant secondary bond market and adoption of international prudential norms for banks and financial institutions would bring consistency and accountability and ensure financial inclusion of all.

In 2008, a relatively good real sector growth despite significant domestic and global adversities, pursuit of prudent monetary measures by the Bangladesh Bank, and supportive fiscal and growth-promoting measures by the government played crucial roles in containing inflationary pressures in Bangladesh relative to many other countries in similar situations. At present, the Bangladesh Bank's monetary policy remains supportive of increased domestic production which is considered to be capable of controlling the demand as well as tackling the current present inflation in the country. Bangladesh is committed to bring down inflation from 10 per cent, keeping in view the complexities of globally transmitted inflation and the need to conditioning perception of inflation in the range of 5.5–6 per cent in the next two to three years so that an inflation rate of around 4.5 per cent can emerge as the medium-term objective. This is needed to ensure the smooth integration of the domestic economy into the global economy and pursue the goal of sustained high growth over the medium-term.

Managing Inflation in South Asia: Key Issues

In the backdrop of rapid globalisation and accelerating economic growth, it is important to identify various channels through which global integration can affect inflation and monetary policies in the South Asian countries. Certainly, greater integration of any economy means that inflation in the domestic economy is more open to pressures coming from outside the country. The general economic argument is that globalisation helps to reduce inflation everywhere. However, in the case of the South Asian countries, this proposition may not be entirely tenable. The reasons lie in many factors, including high import dependence, increased global pressure of excess demand, weak productivity growth in the domestic economy, and persistence of significant structural and institutional rigidities. Moreover, the causalities have country-specific characteristics, including wide variation in relative roles of demand and supply side factors across countries and over different periods in the same country. In addition, the widening internationalisation of inflation in South Asia also means the diminished role of central banks in managing domestic inflation.

In the context of a positive association between excess growth in money supply and inflation, it is held that money supply growth affects growth in real GDP in the first round, while the second round effect is felt by inflation. Therefore, to avoid inflationary pressures in the economy, the formulation of monetary policy needs to be based on a comprehensive consideration of the developments in the real and financial sectors of the economy. Since high growth in money supply can trigger inflationary pressures, it would be important for the central banks to remain cautious about the growth of money supply and its implications on the economy.

A significant issue in adopting appropriate monetary strategy is the relevance of inflation targeting (IT) regime in the South Asian countries. Since the 1990s, IT has emerged as the dominant monetary policy paradigm in several countries — developed and developing countries alike. Many other countries often pursue 'inflation caps' especially in the context of the programs of the International Monetary Fund which can be viewed as a first move toward IT. It is often maintained that IT institutionalises good monetary policy, increases the transparency and accountability of the central bank and provides guideline for other government policies. It also helps to shape private sector expectations that reduce the uncertainty and cost associated with adjustment to low inflation regimes. The gains of IT regime are, however, not well established and there are views that IT may entail several economic costs such as the cost of targeting low inflation, cost of high real interest rate, cost of conflict between IT and balance of payments, and cost of conflict between IT and financial stability. In the South Asian countries, anti-inflation strategy based on IT appears difficult to implement under the present circumstances, especially in view of the problems in fulfilling the institutional requirements for IT, existence of balance of payments vulnerability, and prevalence of shallow financial markets that restrict the sensitivity of interest rate changes in achieving macroeconomic outcomes. Moreover, policies of pursuing low inflation alone may not be desirable in the South Asian countries as this might lock the economies in low employment equilibrium, with consequent adverse impact on poverty.

One of the important functions of the central banks in South Asia is to regulate and supervise the financial system with the views to safeguarding the soundness of the financial system and absorb possible adverse shocks that could be detrimental to economic growth, and improve the efficiency of the financial system and deepen financial intermediation with a view to channeling an increasingly greater volume of financial resources to the productive sectors of the economy. Thus, the vigorous pursuit of developmental and promotional roles, through targeted interventions in the financial sector is important for central banks in South Asia. This, however, need not lead to any compromise on the core objectives of price and financial stability. In order to play desired roles in national development, it is time for the central banks in South Asia to come out of the 'black box' of conventional targets and include employment generation and poverty reduction as key additional objectives.

Finally, the current rapid pace of financial innovation and increasing complexity of cross-border activities pose a substantial challenge for South Asian central banks in ensuring effective monitoring and supervision of the financial sectors in respective countries. This underscores the need to strengthen the framework for cooperation among the central banks and regulatory institutions, including sharing of experiences and expertise to fill critical gaps in information flows and facilitate crisis management. Recognising such needs, financial regulators and central banks of the South Asian Association for Regional Cooperation (SAARC) of eight countries (Afghanistan, Bangladesh, Bhutan, India, Nepal, Maldives, Pakistan and Sri Lanka) have formed the SAARCFINANCE Group in 2002, comprising the Governors of the central banks and the Secretaries of the finance ministries. Besides this, the Asian Clearing Union set up in 1974 by the initiative of the United Nations Economic and Social Commission for Asia and the Pacific for eight countries also plays an important role in settlement of payments of trade among the member countries (Bangladesh, Bhutan, India, Iran, Nepal, Myanmar, Pakistan and Sri Lanka).

Conclusions and Policy Options

The immediate challenge for the central banks in South Asia is to contain the rapidly rising inflationary pressures. The nature and intensity of inflation across countries also vary. In some countries, inflation is largely home-grown, fueled by excessive aggregate demand gathered through years of accommodative monetary policy. For others, domestic supply shocks and global price hikes played the key role and kindled the flames. In view of the complex nature of inflation dynamics in the South Asian countries, the monetary authorities no doubt face a very difficult environment with significant uncertainties surrounding the choice right policies. Moreover, external price shocks that first appeared a few years back are yet to fully pass on to domestic consumers and producers in many countries of the region. Thus, even if international commodity prices ease at present, the pass-through of higher prices will add on to inflation pressures, at least in the near term.

In the present circumstances, direct measures could also play important roles in reducing inflationary pressures in South Asia so that it may not be desirable to leave the burden of keeping inflation at low levels only on demand management policies. With rising food prices, one useful way to dampen the price effects of food supply shocks is to maintain adequate strategic buffer stock of food that could be released when needed through different food transfer programmes targeted at the poor and food insecure households. Keeping in view the financial burden of subsidies in the context of limited fiscal space of the governments, targeted safety nets programmes, feeding programmes for school children, food-for-work programmes, open market sales, and guaranteed employment programme for the poor and disadvantaged households, especially during the lean seasons, could be used in the short run to enhance food entitlements and stabilise prices. Along with mitigating the inflationary impact on the poor through generating short-term employment opportunities and providing access to transfer incomes in the rural areas, it is important to ensure food to the poor at subsidised prices, especially in the urban areas as they do not have any surplus food at home.

At the same time, providing agriculture credit, making input supplies more reliable and relaxing trade policies may bring consumer gain in the short run while providing timely market information would assist the producers to take informed decisions. The thrust of the macro-economic policies should be on increasing domestic production and stabilising supply since the demand of food by the poor is quite inelastic which makes them vulnerable due to the supply variability of food.

In the medium term, responses such as improving institutional capacities and governance structures, including investments in agricultural research, technology, and extension services and in improving trade, marketing, and post-harvest facilities, are the feasible ways of sustaining positive near-term outcomes. Similarly, investment in education and health in rural areas, infrastructure such as irrigation and rural roads, can bring out productivity gains and alleviate the trend of higher prices and food prices in general. At the same time, efforts to stay on inclusive growth path would facilitate policies to address the challenges of rising and high food prices facing the poor.

Obviously, efforts to keep inflation within tolerable limits call for a long-term effort with support of prudent policies. For this, it is important for the South Asian countries to ensure highest sustainable growth in domestic output consistent with price stability that requires a continuous pursuit of supportive macro-economic policies; growth in private sector-led investment; measures to reduce power, transport, and other infrastructure constraints; and a speedy implementation of structural, institutional and financial sector reforms.

In order to restore the South Asian economies to higher growth path over the medium- to long-term, significant efficiency and productivity improvements are required to meet the challenge of limited resources, particularly land (and, thus, food) and fuel. Moreover, effective implementation of country specific reform agendas — that focus on consumers responding to market-oriented price signals on the one hand, and on producers improving efficiency and productivity on the other — are imperative to strengthen competitiveness, foster growth, and generate productive and decent job opportunities. Obviously, moderating inflation and raising economic growth in South Asia require painful trade-offs. However, this should not taken as an excuse for delays in implementing much-needed corrective policy measures to the detriment of both short- and medium-term outlooks. In particular, coordinated monetary and fiscal measures are needed to contain inflation and achieve higher growth for which it would also be desirable to firmly anchor inflation expectations pre-emptively and decisively.

References

ADB (2008). *Asian Development Outlook, April 2008 Update*, Asian Development Bank, Manila.

Bangladesh Bank. *Annual Report*, various years, Bangladesh Bank, Dhaka.

BBS. *CPI and Rate of Inflation*, Bangladesh Bureau of Statistics, Dhaka, Ministry of Planning, Government of the People's Republic of Bangladesh.

BBS (2007). *Report of the Household Income and Expenditure Survey 2005*, Bangladesh Bureau of Statistics, Dhaka, Ministry of Planning, Government of the People's Republic of Bangladesh.

Bruno, M. (1995). Does Inflation Really Lower Growth? *Finance and Development*, 32(3).

Bruno, M. and W. Easterly (1996). Inflation and Growth: In Search of a Stable Relationship, *Federal Reserve Bank of St. Louis Review*, May–June 1996.

FAO (2008). *Soaring Food Prices: Facts, Perspectives, Impacts and Actions Required*, Report prepared for the High-Level Conference on World Food Security: The Challenges of Climate Change and Bioenergy, 3–5 June 2000, Food and Agriculture Organization, Rome.

Fischer, S. (1993). The Role of Macroeconomic Factors in Growth, *Journal of Monetary Economics*, 32, 485–512.

Garuda, G. (2000). The Distributional Effects of IMF Programs: A Cross-Country Analysis, *World Development*, 28.

IMF (2008). *World Economic Outlook October 2008: Financial Stress, Downturns, and Recoveries*, International Monetary Fund, Washington DC.

Ivanic, M. and W. Martin (2008). *Implications of Higher Global Food Prices for Poverty in Low Income Countries*, Policy Research Working Paper 4594, Development Research Group, World Bank, April 2008, Washington D.C.

Mishkin, F.S. (2004). *The Economics of Money, Banking and Financial Markets*, Seventh Edition, Columbia University Press, New York.

Mortaza, M.G. and S. Hasnayen (2008). Inflation Accounting Across Income Groups: Does Inflation Hurt the Poor More in Bangladesh? PN 0807, *Bangladesh Bank Quarterly*, 5(3), January–March 2008.

Mujeri, M.K., M.G. Mortaza, and M. Shahiduzzaman (2008). *Trend and Characteristics of Inflation in Bangladesh*, Policy Paper No. 0901, Policy Analysis Unit, Bangladesh Bank, Dhaka.

Chapter 6

'Going Places'? Emerging Issues on the Diaspora and Indian International Economic Activity

Peter Reeves

Migration has been a key element in the development of South Asia since the early 19th century. From early times, traders from South Asia had moved to trading areas in Central Asia, Southeast Asia and around the Indian Ocean. Internally, peasants and artisans migrated to areas where there was land to be acquired, where there was a demand for their services or where more amenable governance was available. However, with the development of new forms of plantation agriculture (such as tea plantations in Assam) and new industrial areas (such as Bombay (now Mumbai) and Calcutta (now Kolkata)) in the 19th century, peasants from many poorer areas of the subcontinent moved to find work on plantations or in the new mills, railway workshops and the like.

The same was true, externally, in the 19th century as peasants were recruited from less well-developed regions of northern, southern and western India for the indenture system that was needed to provide labour for colonial areas of plantation production (for example, of sugar in the Caribbean islands, Fiji and Mauritius; rubber in Malaya; and tea in Ceylon). This emigration to new colonial areas under indenture lasted from the 1830s to the 1920s and provided the basis for the development of what is generally termed the 'old diaspora' of Indian communities. After the Second World War (1939–45) and the decolonisation process in South Asia, labour migration to the United Kingdom began the process of building the 'new diaspora'

93

which grew in importance in the later 20th century with large increases in professional migration to the United States, Europe and areas of the Commonwealth such as Australia, New Zealand and Canada.

Another area of migration which had important implications for the economies of the South Asian states was the major movement of people into the new dominions of India and Pakistan following the Partition of India in 1947 when as many as 18 million moved to find new homes in the two independent dominions. Other movements also followed decolonisation in other parts of South Asia — pressures on Indians located in Burma (now Myanmar) to return to India; attempts by the new government of Ceylon (now Sri Lanka) to have Tamil tea workers repatriated to southern India; large increases in migration between Nepal and India; and migration from East Pakistan to India at the time of the fighting which led to the formation of Bangladesh in 1971 (and of which there are still echoes in Bangladeshi movements in eastern India). Similarly, there are questions posed by Nepalese migration to Bhutan.

There are, therefore, a number of areas in which 'emerging issues on migration' could (and need) to be considered. This chapter will focus on issues related to activities in the diaspora, as it has developed in the late 20th and early 21st centuries.

This chapter looks, firstly, at the way in which Indian entrepreneurs, using 'acquisition and merger' activity, found scope for their industrial development skills in a period when there had been significant changes in the context in which the international economy operated. It will then look at India's reassessment of the role of diasporic entrepreneurs in the light of those changes — especially the role of the Non-Resident Indians (NRIs) after the economic 'reforms' of the early 1990s. As Professor Binod Khadria has put it, Indian assessment of the NRI involvement through the diaspora in the international economic system has moved from a judgement of 'brain drain' to 'brain gain'.[1]

---

[1] Khadria, B. (2006). 'Postwar Migration' and 'The Migration of Professionals', In Brij V. Lal, Peter Reeves and Rajesh Rai (eds.), *The Encyclopedia of the Indian Diaspora* [*hereafter EID*], pp. 66–75. Khadria, B. (2006b). 'Indian Professionals Turned Entrepreneurs', in *EID*, pp. 80–81. See also Rai, R. (2006). 'Business and Entrepreneurship', in *EID*, pp. 77, 79.

He argues that, as a result, the Indian state has come to realise that the NRIs could have considerable importance in India's growth as an economic superpower. The last section will then look at the further internationalising of the Indian corporate sector by expansionary activity by Indian corporations in the international economy through the' acquisition and mergers' system.

The period that we are concerned with runs from the mid-1980s to the first decade of the 21st century. From the mid-1980s, there were a series of unparalleled changes in the international state system stemming from political changes in the Soviet Union; the disintegration of the Union of Soviet Socialist Republics (USSR); the end of Soviet power in Eastern Europe; and the expansion of the European Union and the opening of new economic opportunities in eastern Europe. These developments were felt very acutely in the South Asian states, especially India, which had developed close relations and economic ties with the USSR, following the 1971 war with Pakistan over the emergence of Bangladesh. Conflict then arose in the Gulf region of the Middle East with the Iraqi invasion of Kuwait, which prompted the United States and its allies to confront Saddam Hussein and to open the first Gulf War. The impact of this on oil supplies and on the Middle Eastern economies and labour markets brought new hardship to the South Asian states through increases in the price of oil; the closure of the labour markets in the Middle East; a consequent loss of remittance income; and the return of most migrant workers to South Asia for the period of the war.

In the case of India, the limited steps taken to 'liberalise' the Indian economic system in the 1980s were replaced by major 'reforms' carried out in 1991–92 by the new Congress-led government of Prime Minister Narasimha Rao. These sweeping economic reforms, calculated to meet the International Monetary Fund's call for India to '... deflate, devalue, denationalise and deregulate...'[2] came to India in 1991–92 as a result of both the new global economy following the release of

---

[2] Stern, R.W. (1993). *Changing India. Bourgeois Revolution on the Subcontinent,* (EDM, Singapore) p. 219, Cambridge University Press, Cambridge.

Eastern Europe and the collapse of the Soviet Union in 1989 and events in the Middle East which affected remittance incomes and increased the price of oil. The major reform initiative changed the model from Import Substitution Industrialisation (ISI) to export-oriented industrialisation. The 'reforms' produced important changes in relation to the Indian economy and India's interactions in the global trading system.

Although it was not noted at the time, the first players in the international arena were, in fact, Indian entrepreneurs operative outside India who were quick the see that these conditions opened possibilities for them, not in terms of the diaspora but rather in opening transnational space within which they could turn the new conditions in their favour. Two interesting examples of this taking up of opportunities in the 1990s were Dr Sudhir Gupta who, through his firm, Amtel Holdings, became a major tyre manufacturer and trader in Russia;[3] and Lakshmi Narayan Mittal who built Mittal Steel into a worldwide steel corporation.

Gupta completed 11 years of tertiary education in the USSR just as Mikhail Gorbachev's campaigns for '*Perestroika*' and '*Glasnost*' ushered in (as he described it) 'a free-for-all capitalist economy'. Instead of returning to India, he gained four years experience as the Director of an Indian-owned store in Moscow. He then founded Amtel and identified the Russian rubber industry as a possible niche for

---

[3] Reeves, P. (2008). 'An Entrepreneurial Diaspora? Transnational Space and India's International Economic Expansion', in Rajesh, R. and P. Reeves (eds.), *The South Asian Diaspora: Transnational Networks and Changing Identities*, pp. 57–68; Reeves, P. (2006). Dr Sudhir Gupta, in *EID*, p. 78. These articles draw on: Noorani, M. (2005a). Interview: Sudhir Gupta, President — Amtel Tyres, *Indian Rubber Journal*, Vol. 90, pp. 10–12; Noorani, M. (2005b). 'The Rise and Rise of Dr Sudhir Gupta's Amtel Tyres', *Indian Rubber Journal/International Rubber Journal*, Vol. 90, pp. 14–20; *People of Indian Origin* (2005). Turning Point: The Titan of the Tyre Biz', Vol. 1, No. 3, pp. 10–14; White, L. (2004a). Amtel Invests $100m to Make 20m Tyres by 2006, *European Rubber Journal*, Vol. 186, No. 3, pp. 11–12; White, L. (2004b). Amtel-Nokian Tyres Deal, *European Rubber Journal*, Vol. 186, No. 3, p. 13.

Amtel. Working initially with Soviet government agencies and then directly with Russian manufacturers following the collapse of the Soviet Union, he built up an annual import trade of 100,000 tonnes through Amtel.

He then expanded Amtel's activities from the mid-1990s. He diversified Amtel, firstly, in 1994 into packaging; and then into petrochemical production. Between 1997 and 1999, Gupta acquired several Russian tyre plants and expanded their range by developing facilities for the production of carbon black and nylon tyre cord, which were key accompaniments to tyre manufacture. These developments were brought to a new level in 2001–02 when Amtel both integrated its product supply and retail systems and then upgraded its infrastructure to provide the technological base for higher quality production. At this stage Amtel, specialising in middle range tyre products, was the second or third largest Russian tyre company.

Gupta then began to look for collaboration with manufacturers outside Russia in order to broaden Amtel's product and trading range. This led him, in 2005, to acquire Vredestein Bandan B. V., a leading tyre producer and trader in the Netherlands for €195.6 million. His plants employed 27,000 workers and staff. The new firm was then able, building on Vredestein's international trading networks, to place itself as an internationally significant 'brand' at the middle and upper ends of the market. In June 2005, Amtel Vredestein offered shares on the London Stock Exchange. By 2006, about ten per cent of Amtel share capital was held by institutional investors, including Citicorp International Finance Corporation which had 4.1 per cent. By private placement, US$70 million were invested by Alfa-Bank (the largest private commercial bank in Russia) and Temasek Holdings (a major investment arm of the Singapore government and its 'Government-Linked Companies'). As one commentator put it, Gupta's 'rise and rise' was clear for all to see.

Mittal became well-known in the 1990s for his success in building a formidable steel 'empire', which he capped off in great style in 2006 when he successfully led Mittal Steel's takeover of the newly-refurbished Arcelor Steel, which was Europe's most important steel maker.[4]

In 1976, after experience in the Kolkata steel mill in which his father was a partner, Mittal was sent to Indonesia to manage a mill, Ispat Indo, which the family had acquired. This move provided the experience that enabled Mittal to set up his own operation in 1994. Over the next decade, Mittal built a world-wide steel production conglomerate, which became Mittal Steel in 2004. He targeted under-producing or failing steel works, mainly in developing and unsettled areas across the globe, which could be acquired at low cost and then be turned around by Mittal's high-powered Indian management teams on an 'integrated mini-mill' model. This strategy enabled Mittal to consolidate a substantial position in the world steel industry with two steel-producing firms, Ispat International NV and his family's privately controlled LNM Group. These two firms came to operate worldwide holdings in Trinidad and Tobago, Mexico, Canada, the United States, Ireland, the Czech Republic, Poland, Macedonia, Romania, Kazakhstan, Ukraine and South Africa.

In 2004, Mittal Steel NV emerged from a merger of Ispat International, the LNM Group and the United States-based International Steel. Mittal Steel NV was registered in Rotterdam but managed from London and the Mittal family (Mittal, his wife and two children, Aditya and Vanisha) held 88 per cent of its stock.

The most important steel works in Europe, Arcelor, had been formed by a merger in 2002 of three leading European steel manufacturers

---

[4] Reeves, P. (2008). 'An Entrepreneurial Diaspora? Transnational Space and India's International Economic Expansion', in Rajesh, R. and P. Reeves (eds.), *The South Asian Diaspora: Transnational Networks and Changing Identities*, pp. 57–68, Routledge, London. This article draws upon: Fenby, J. (2006). 'Europe's Globalisation Dilemma, *Straits Times*, 5 June 2006, p. 17; Girdharidas, A. (2006a). 'French Elites Raise Spectre of India Threat', *Business Times* (Singapore), 6 February 2006, p. 15 (reprinted from *International Herald Tribune*); Giridharadas, A. (2006b). 'Following Mittal's Footsteps Overseas', *Business Times*, 15 February 2006, p. 14 (reprinted from *International Herald Tribune*); Gumble, P. (2006). 'Nerves of Steel', *Time*, 13 February 2006, pp. 22–25; *Time* (2006b). 'Lakshmi Mittal', *Time*, 13 November 2006, p. 73.

based in France, Spain and Luxembourg. In 2006, Mittal identified it as an ideal target for merger with Mittal Steel, so that Mittal–Arcelor would have the complete range of steel products. He raised this possibility of a merger with the Arcelor Chief Executive Officer (CEO), Guy Dollé, who flatly rejected the suggestion. On 26 January 2006, therefore, Mittal announced that Mittal Steel would make a hostile bid for Arcelor, which would value the company at US$23.3 billion; the offer was four Mittal Steel shares, plus a cash payment of €35.25, for each five Arcelor shares.[5]

The immediate response by the Arcelor Board and the related European governments was, in the *Economist*'s words, 'patriotic outrage'.[6] Mittal confronted this hostility and the attempts to denigrate the value and purpose of the bid by releasing plans for the development of a 'steel powerhouse', which would produce 130 million tonnes of steel annually, three times the production of Nippon Steel, the world's largest producer. Mittal toured Western Europe talking with governments and bureaucrats and moved around the continent to meet and talk with Arcelor's shareholders. By mid-March 2006, the press was reporting, 'It is clear that the shareholders want this transaction'.[7]

On 29 January 2006, the Arcelor Board unanimously rejected the Mittal bid and continued to disparage Mittal Steel as 'an Indian company' which did not have the strength to be a realistic bidder or competitor. The Arcelor Board was prepared to increase dividends for shareholders from €1.2 to €1.85 and it offered €5.00 per share

---

[5] Reeves, P. (2008). 'An Entrepreneurial Diaspora? Transnational Space and India's International Economic Expansion', in Rajesh, R. and P. Reeves (eds.), *The South Asian Diaspora: Transnational Networks and Changing Identities*, pp. 57–68, Routledge, London. See also Bouquet, T. (2007a). 'Inside the World of the Men of Steel, *Evening Standard* (London)', 11 September; Bouquet, T. (2007b). 'Man of Steel', *The Australian Magazine*, 24–25 November, pp. 22–23, 25–26, 29; Tim, B. and B. Ousey (2008). *Cold Steel. Britain's Richest Man and the Multi-Billion Dollar Battle for a Global Empire*; Lee Little Brown, London & New York; *Business Times* (2006). Arcelor-Mittal a giant with 10 per cent market share, 27 June, p. 19.
[6] Cross-border mergers: Heavy Mittal, *Economist*, 4 February 2006, pp. 11–12.
[7] *Business Times* (Singapore), 17 March 2006, p. 13.

for a share buy-back. The Board also made overtures in a bid to a Russian steelmaker, Severstal, with the objective of placing an expanded Arcelor beyond Mittal's reach. In mid-May 2006, the bid which Mittal had put on the table in late January 2006 was finally cleared for serious discussion by the regulating authorities in the United States, the European Union and the most closely involved European states — the Netherlands, France, Luxembourg and Spain. The formal bid was launched on 18 May 2006. The offer for five Arcelor shares remained four Mittal shares plus €35.25; however, the total value of the bid now valued Arcelor at US$33.7 billon, which was a substantial increase on the original bid of US$23.3 billion. On 11 June 2006, the Arcelor Board formally rejected the Mittal offer and made a last desperate attempt to foil it with another move involving Severstal. This was seen by some commentators as a cunning move to outflank Mittal, but others saw it as a very risky strategy and there was strong shareholder opposition to it from the beginning. On 30 June 2006, shareholders rejected the Severstal deal outright and the Board had to recommend acceptance of the Mittal bid.

The acceptance of the bid by the shareholders opened the way for changes in management. Dollé left the CEO's position immediately and another Director, Roland Junck, became CEO. However, in November 2006, Junck resigned to make way for Mittal to take over as CEO of Arcelor–Mittal, in addition to his position as President.[8]

The approach and the *modus operandi* of Gupta and Mittal broke with earlier patterns of operation. They used their diasporic position

---

[8] This campaign for Arcelor can be followed in a series of articles in the *Economist*: Cross-border mergers: Heavy Mittal, 4 February 2006, pp. 11–12; Steel: Age of Giants, 4 February 2006, pp. 55–56; European Takeovers: Powerless Patriots, 4 February 2006, pp. 56–57; Economic Nationalism: From Karl Marx's copybook', 4 March 2006, p. 12; The Nationalist Resurgence, 4 March 2006, p. 49; European Takeovers: To the Barricades, 4 March 2006, pp. 55–56; Arcelor: Up in Arms, 29 April 2006, pp. 62–63; Can India fly, 3 June 2006, p. 11; Treating Shareholders as Pig Iron, 3 June 2006, pp. 68–69; Don't Touch Taittinger, 3 June 2006, p. 69; Steel Takeovers: Cast Iron, 17 June 2006, p. 13; Arcelor Wobbles, 17 June 2006, p. 72; India's Acquisition Game: Circle the Wagons, 14 October 2006, pp. 72–4.

when they needed to, but they also appeared to be able to act more independently, both of the diaspora and the homeland. It is in this way that they can be seen as occupying a 'transnational', space in which they are much freer of external controllers who would be in a position to limit their freedom of action.

This meant greater freedom from the restrictive Indian regulations and practices of the 'permit-quota-licence Raj'. Such freedom meant being able to marshal financial support from institutions such as stock exchanges and banks with broader entrepreneurial objectives than might be available in India (an example was the European Bank for Reconstruction and Development, which Mittal used for acquisitions in eastern Europe). Having 'freedom from regulations' necessarily meant that there was less scope for contact with governmental, bureaucratic and political elements for operations within India, but this could probably be discounted because one of the incentives of operating independently was precisely to avoid competition with established business and financial players who had already successfully established themselves in the operational world of the 'licence Raj'.

Both Gupta and Mittal gave the impression that they did not need Indian support in terms of operating at this international level. They appeared to be not thinking in terms of being 'Indian' but rather of being straightforwardly international entrepreneurs, and from this, we might take the point that, in the case of such entrepreneurs, we need think less about identification with 'India' and more about the skills which they had acquired operating in transnational space and building their 'empires'.

Nonetheless, entrepreneurial activity was seen as adding to India's international economic expansion. For instance, in New Delhi in July 2006, once the bid had proved to be successful, Mittal himself talked about why Indian support — while not specific to the deal — had been important. He indicated that he believed that failure to carry through the takeover would have been 'a setback for Indian businessmen'. Subsequent events during this July visit suggested that there might also be a sense in which these 'defensive' moves were linked to that wider agenda of encouraging the NRIs' participation in the Indian economy. For example, Mittal, having announced that there would be 'no [more] acquisition fireworks this year' turned his attention quickly to plans for major investments in steel mills in Jharkhand and Orissa, which may well have been part of a 'deal' with India. Was the government of India thinking in terms of greater liaison with diaspora entrepreneurs coming back into India — as Indian firms moved out into international space?

Perhaps, the fact is that the liberalisation of post-1991 in India opened more widely the gates for relatively independent entrepreneurial activity by Indians. When Gupta and Mittal began, perhaps those opportunities were not available except by striking out on an independent entrepreneurial path of one's own choosing. By 2006–07, however, even within India, such moves could be made by corporations or individuals and the Indian state was able to accommodate such players within a general understanding of the role and scope to be allowed (even encouraged?) among NRIs? If this is the case, we will need to look at developments in the next decade of India–NRI interaction to see the full force of such a development. If such a development does take place, it will help to underline the importance, in parallel to the economic liberalising process in India, of the work and skills of the Indian entrepreneurs who chose to operate in 'transnational economic space' from the 1980s onwards.

The success of Gupta and Mittal indicated that Indian entrepreneurs operating as 'international players' could succeed in the international marketplace. What also became clear is that the combination of liberalisation and a more open international 'space' made it possible for there to be greater recognition of diasporic entrepreneurs as valuable to Indian development. Diasporic entrepreneurs — previously largely disregarded — came into clearer focus because their experience, capital, skills and contacts can be seen as valuable to India.

Thus, while international 'acquisition and mergers' became an important part of India's international economic expansion from 2000 onwards, the Indian 'entrepreneurs of transnational space' had already been moving in this direction from the late 1980s and early 1990s. What they established were not 'Indian' firms, since they had no Indian home base or connection, but rather international firms led by Indians. However, as we see in the case of Mittal Steel, identification as an 'Indian firm' was often applied because situations arose when an Indian entrepreneur (even without national backing) was highly competitive and rivals had to have some 'identity' to call into question. Moreover, it was also a fact that, on occasions, the government of India treated some of these firms (Mittal Steel was a prime example) as if they *were* Indian companies.

The commercial success of many Indian migrants to the post-war United Kingdom and the growth of professional migration from South Asia from the 1960s onward — especially to the United States and Canada — ensured that South Asia's entrepreneurial talent: was well recognised in the later 20th century in those advanced economies. The well-trained graduates of the Indian Institutes of Technology, the Regional Engineering Colleges, the medical schools and the Indian Institutes of Managements, as well as those from the subcontinent who went to British and United States universities gave the 'new diaspora' a markedly different profile to the 'old diaspora'. In major developments such as 'Silicon Valley', where the information, communication and technology revolution was nurtured, Indian engineering, entrepreneurial and managerial talent was very obvious. Moreover, Indian scientific and research capacity was also strongly evident in the last decades of the 20th century, even while economic development under the 'permit-licence-quota Raj' seemed slow and unsure.

However, while the fate of Indians in the diaspora had been of concern to Indian nationalist forces during the later decades of colonial rule in India, once independence was gained in 1947, the diaspora was not seen as having any great importance for the newly-independent nation. In part, this was because of the way in which India approached its own national development. Led by Jawaharlal Nehru and working through the Planning Commission, India chose ISI as the basis for the socialist planned economic development that the state — given its role on the 'commanding heights of the economy' — would bring about. Effectively ISI was focussed on domestic change: India would industrialise using its own resources and people. In such a scheme, there was no role seen for the people of the diaspora; they were in some ways recognisably 'Indian' but they were not in India and they were people with a new identity forged in their new homeland. Moreover, those who left to work and settle in Britain or the United States in the post-war migration were effectively seen as 'leaving' for their own benefit and not 'participating' in the homeland's great task. They were, as they were dubbed, NRIs.

By the later 1990s, however, the Indian government began to work and plan for a greater recognition of the NRIs who were now seen as those who could help to bring about development that was desired. Their 'non-resident' status could now be seen not as 'non-participation' but as the necessary training for the tasks in hand. In 2000, a 'High Level Committee' chaired by L.M. Singhvi recommended the creation of a 'Department of Overseas Indian Affairs' and a new celebration to recognize the NRI contribution, the *'Pravasi Bharatiya Divas'*, which was tellingly to be held each year on 9 January, which was the precise day on which Mahatma Gandhi had returned to India after his 23 year sojourn in South Africa. More pertinently still, there were incentives offered to NRIs to return to India, to include India in their business plans and — most usefully — to invest directly in Indian ventures and to bring their managerial and entrepreneurial skills to bear on developments in India. Diaspora experience was seen to have direct value to India's plans for dramatic economic development.[9]

In this new attitude to the diaspora, there was some recognition that not all members of the Indian diasporic communities had been businessmen and women or successful entrepreneurs. Despite success stories from Surinam, Fiji and Mauritius, where the Indian communities had gained some political and social power from their demographic growth and business acumen, many, especially from the 'old diaspora', were poor and had limited means and ambitions. It was, nonetheless, important that the diaspora as a whole was drawn closer to the 'homeland', especially as many people of Indian descent living in diasporic communities began to show an interest in being associated with India as it rose in importance internationally and in many areas there was a spontaneous growth of organisations for 'people of Indian origin'.

---

[9] On these developments, see Kudaisya, G. 'Indian Leadership and the Diaspora', in *EID*, pp. 82–89.

As a result, the gathering-in of the diaspora did recognise such 'People of Indian Origin' for whom special passports and the like were provided, while still establishing an implicit hierarchy that preserved the importance of the NRIs. (One might even wonder if the acronym was now read as 'Newly-Rediscovered Indians'.)

In addition to recognising the skills of entrepreneurs such as Gupta and Mittal and recruiting more firmly the support of entrepreneurs from the diaspora, India's international economic expansion was seen by the turn of the century to involve major Indian corporations: those corporations began to see advantages in 'acquisitions and mergers' and, over the first decade of the 21st century, there is an impressive international expansion of corporate India. The result, since 2000–01, has been an increasing interest in the expansion of India's place and role in the international economy by major Indian domestic industrial corporations. This has led to the adoption by India's leading industrial and trading houses of a new international strategy involving the acquisition of foreign industrial and commercial concerns to strengthen India's position in the global economy. In 2005, Indian companies purchased 118 firms at a total cost of US$2.91 billion.[10] That was seven times the amount spent in 2001, when these moves were first getting under way. At these levels, Indian-led 'acquisition and merger' activity was small in international terms — the 2005 purchases were a mere one per cent of global merger activity, but in terms of India's economic opening up, it was a highly significant portent after five decades of ISI-dominated economic progress. The figures for just the first three quarters of 2006 — when 115 acquisitions were made at a cost of US$7.4 billion — was an indication of the expanding pace of acquisition activity. In 2007, a new peak was reached when Tata Steel paid US$13 billion to secure the Anglo–Dutch steelmaker, Corus.[11] In October,

---

[10] *Business Times*, 6 February 2006, p. 15.

[11] *The Australian*, 5–6 May 2007, p. 39. Engadio, P. 'The Last Rajah *Business Week*', 13 August 2007, accessed at: http://www.businessweek.com/magazine/content/07_33/b4046045.htm?chan=search; Tata and Corus: Steely Logic, *Economist*, 28 October 2006, pp. 80–81.

the *Economist* reported, moreover, that this international activity had not weakened India's domestic investment since the outflow of capital almost equalled inflow.[12] Commentators on the Indian economy predict that the acquisition strategy would see Indian firms become 'truly global' in the next 'five to seven' years.[13]

---

[12] 'India's Acquisition Game: Circle the Wagons', *Economist*, 14 October 2006, pp. 72–74.
[13] *Business Times*, 6 February 2006, p. 15.

Chapter 7

India's Soft Power and Cultural Influence

Bibek Debroy

Culture is a difficult term to define. Etymologically, it is derived from the Latin *cultura*, which means to tend, cultivate or till. Thus, agriculture is an older use than culture in the sense of art, beliefs, institutions, rituals, religion, language, law and morality. In its universal declaration on cultural diversity, the United Nation Educational, Scientific and Cultural Organisation effectively defined culture as "the set of distinctive spiritual, material, intellectual and emotional features of society or a social group, and that it encompasses, in addition to art and literature, lifestyles, ways of living together, value systems, traditions and beliefs".[1] India is a large country. It is a heterogeneous country. In the absence of a common language and common religion, culture is difficult to define in the Indian context. There are sub-cultures within the country and there is a great deal of syncretism and cultural pluralism. Nor should any discussion on India's cultural influence be restricted to post-Independence India. By its very construct, culture is not constrained by confines of political and administrative processes and decisions, and is reflective of the greater Indian subcontinent. In that sense of diffusion down the ages, there are elements of architecture, music, dance, theatre, films, art, literature, cuisine, attire, sports and religion, all of which have crossed borders.

---

[1] *Universal Declaration on Cultural Diversity*, UNESCO, 21 February 2002, http://www.unesco.org/education/imld_2002/unversal_decla.shtml.

In contrast to cultural influence, soft power, as a term, is of relatively recent vintage and is identified both with Joseph Nye[2] and with the American influence. "What about soft power? The basic concept of power is the ability to influence others to get them to do what you want. There are three major ways to do that: one is to threaten them with sticks; the second is to pay them with carrots; the third is to attract them or co-opt them, so that they want what you want. If you can get others to be attracted, to want what you want, it costs you much less in carrots and sticks."[3] In a different day and age, this is reminiscent of Kautilya's[4] *Arthashastra*, particularly the ninth chapter, where there is a reference to *sama* (conciliation or pacification), *dana* (gifts), *danda* (coercion, punishment or force) and *bheda* (dissension). In that jargon, the point being made is that *sama* results from cultural influences and is cheaper and more effective than *dana*, *danda* and *bheda*. And if *sama* is successful, the other three options may well be unnecessary. For instance, "No two countries that both had McDonald's had fought a war against each other since each got its McDonald's."[5] Friedman's assertion was not meant to be a blanket assertion and was more suggestive. Depending on how one defines war, countries that had McDonald's have gone to war, Russia and Georgia are but one instance.

Down the years, India's influence in the region has been considerable, often in ways we are not even aware of. The name Canon is a case in point, derived from Avalokiteshvara.[6] Avalokiteshvara means the lord who looks down and is probably pre-Buddhist in origin. In Sanskrit, it is easy to confuse letters that are similar and

---

[2] Especially the books *The Paradox of American Power* (2002), *Soft Power: The Means to Succeed in World Politics* (2004), *The Power Game: A Washington Novel* (2004) and *Understanding International Conflicts*, 6th edition, (2006).

[3] Joseph Nye's interview with Joanne Myers, http://www.cceia.org/resources/transcripts/4466.html.

[4] Possibly between 350 and 283 BCE.

[5] Friedman, T. L. (1999). *The Lexus and the Olive Tree.*

[6] Nayan Chanda (2007). *Bound Together: How Traders, Preachers, Warriors and Adventurers Shaped Globalization*, Nayan Chanda, Yale University Press, briefly mentions this interesting derivation.

Avalokiteshvara may well have been Avalokitesvara, meaning the lord who has perceived sound. In Buddhism, Avalokitesvara became originally identified with the Bodhisattva[7] and the name was translated into Chinese as Guan Yin and into Japanese as Kwannon or Kwanon. The Precision Optical Instruments Laboratory was established in Japan in 1930 by Goro Yoshida and his brother-in-law and the former happened to be a Buddhist. Therefore, not only did the company's 1934 logo display the Kwanon and the camera was also sold under that name. Finally, in 1937, the company's name was changed to Canon.

"My thanks, also, to some of the speakers on this platform who, referring to the delegates from the Orient, have told you that these men from far-off nations may well claim the honor of bearing to different lands the idea of toleration. I am proud to belong to a religion which has taught the world both tolerance and universal acceptance." That is a quote from Swami Vivekananda's welcome address at the World Parliament of Religions in Chicago in September 1893. This becomes relevant in defining an Indian identity, since such an identity is not easy to define in the absence of a common religion or language. Any attempt to construct such an identity would perforce have to build on a strong sense of religion[8] and elements of tolerance and non-violence. It is not quite the case that India has never practiced hard power — the Chola and to a lesser extent the Pandyan empires are counter-examples. However, such exceptions are rare. The practice of soft power was more common and pervasive, driven by both commercial and religious considerations. Maritime trade routes connected India with East Asia and Rome. There was a spice route via Africa and India was also on the southern part of the silk route. Trade and religious missionaries both used the same routes. And with the exception of Ashoka and, to a lesser extent, Kanishka neither flow was state-driven. Indeed, soft power works best when it is not

---

[7] The nuance varies across Mahayana, Theravada and Vajrayana, but we need not get into that.

[8] As opposed to any specific religion. Alternatively, one might wish to use the term spiritualism.

state-driven. Until recent times, Indian soft power was identified with religious overtones — Sri Aurobindo, Chinmayananda, Dayanand Saraswati, Guru Nanak Dev, Gyaneshwar, Sant Kabir, Maharishi Mahesh Yogi, Anandamayi Ma, Osho Rajneesh, Paramahansa Yogananda, Ramakrishna Paramahansa, Sathya Sai Baba, Shirdi Sai Baba, Swami Sivananda, Sri Sri Ravi Shankar, Swami Vivekananda and assorted practitioners of *yoga*. This certainly did not mean that this influence was only restricted to the Indian diaspora. Invariably, it transcended the diaspora. Though not quite the same, one should also mention the influence of Mahatma Gandhi, imported by South Africa as Mohandas Karamchand Gandhi and re-exported with significant value addition as Mahatma Gandhi. Gandhi has influenced and inspired Martin Luther King, James Lawson, Nelson Mandela, Khan Abdul Ghaffar Khan, Steve Biko and Aung San Suu Kyi.

The post-1991 economic reforms and India's growing economic clout de-linked Indian soft power from the historical religious overtones. This is now reminiscent of American soft power and is a phenomenon that has also occurred in China.

Figures on languages spoken globally are somewhat unreliable, since they typically include native speakers and do not include those who speak the language as a second language. Subject to this, Mandarin is the most widely spoken language in the world, with a range of speakers between 873 million and 1.2 billion.[9] Hindi or Hindustani comes next, with a range between 366 million and 650 million, the upper end of the range resulting from the inclusion of Urdu and secondary language speakers. English, Bengali, Punjabi, Telugu, Marathi and Tamil also figure in the top-20 languages of the world. If one includes all speakers of English, including second and third languages, 1,143 million people speak English. Of these, the United Kingdom accounts for 59.6 million. The United States

---

[9] These figures are from http://en.wikipedia.org/wiki/List_of_languages_by_number_of_native_speakers.

(215.4 million), India (90 million) and Nigeria (79 million) are ahead of the United Kingdom. Other than its implications for business-process outsourcing and knowledge-process outsourcing, this knowledge of English has led to several Indian (or of Indian ethnic origins) authors writing with great felicity in English — Dhan Gopal Mukerji (Newberry Medal in 1928), Raja Rao, Nirad C. Chaudhuri, R. K. Narayan, Mulk Raj Anand, Khuswant Singh, Salman Rushdie (Booker 1981, Booker of Bookers 1992, Best of Bookers 2008), Bharati Mukherjee, Vikram Seth (Commonwealth Writers Prize, 1994), Anita Desai, Ruth Prawer Jhabvala (Booker 1975), Kiran Desai (Booker 2006), Arundhati Roy (Booker 1997), Chitra Banerjee Divakurni, Raj Kamal Jha, Jhumpa Lahiri (Pulitzer Prize 2000), Amit Chaudhuri, Suketu Mehta, Amitav Ghosh, Vikas Swarup, Rohinton Mistry, David Davidar, Upamanyu Chatterjee, Aravind Adiga (Booker 2008) and the third generation Indian V. S. Naipaul (Booker 1971, Nobel Prize 2001). This changes India's image in subtle and not so subtle ways.

So does the film and television industry. In the last few years, India has produced the largest number of feature films in the world, with 1,164 films produced in 2007.[10] The United States came second with 453, Japan third with 407 and China fourth with 402.[11] Indian film production is usually equated with Hindi-language Bollywood, often described as the largest film-producing centre in the world. Bollywood films are watched in South Asia (Afghanistan, Bangladesh, Nepal, Pakistan and Sri Lanka), the Middle East (Saudi Arabia, United Arab Emirates, Oman, Kuwait, Bahrain, Qatar, Palestine and Jordan), Africa (Somalia, Nigeria, Syria, Egypt, Mauritius, Kenya and Senegal), Eastern Europe (Russia), Western Europe (Britain, Germany, France and Scandinavia), the Americas (the United States, Canada and the Caribbean) and Oceania (Australia, New Zealand and Fiji).

---

[10] http://www.afc.gov.au/gtp/acompfilms.html.
[11] Ticket sales are higher for Bollywood than for Hollywood, though revenue figures are much more for the latter.

They are sometimes dubbed in local languages and viewership is not restricted to the diaspora. One often tends to forget that several Bollywood-related awards (Bollywood Movie Awards, Global Indian Film Awards, and the International Indian Film Academy Awards.[12] Awards and Zee Cine Awards) are held overseas, films are shot in overseas locations, technical work is out-sourced, films are watched through cable television and digital video disk routes and there is the occasional foreign actor or actress who has featured in Bollywood films.[13] Similar effects exist for television serials and Bollywood songs and song-based contest programmes and the odd Indian choreographer and music composer has now been hired for Broadway and Hollywood. While Bollywood stories and music have borrowed liberally from Hollywood, *Munnabhai MBBS* is now being remade in Hollywood. However, one should not equate the Indian film industry with Bollywood alone. There is the Kannada (Sandalwood), Bengali (Tollywood),[14] Assamese, Tamil (Kollywood),[15] Malayalam, Marathi, Oriya (Ollywood) and Punjabi (Pollywood) film industry too. Ismail Merchant, who died in 2005, was a director many in North America and Western Europe would have identified with.

India has a strong classical music tradition.[16] Despite this tradition having interacted with Western music through exponents like Ustad Ali Akbar Khan and Pandit Ravi Shankar and resulting in fusion, often of the rock and roll variety, this trend did not really become mainstream, transcending the diaspora. The mainstreaming occurred largely because of popular or film music, with Bhangra thrown in.[17]

---

[12] This was held in Singapore in 2004.

[13] Alice Patten in *Rang De Basanti*, several in *Kisna, Lagaan, The Rising: Ballad of Mangal Pandey*, Kseniya Ryabinkina in *Mera Naam Joker* and Tania Zaetta in *Salaam Namaste* are examples.

[14] Watched in Bangladesh, which has its own Dollywood.

[15] Watched in Sri Lanka, Singapore, Malaysia, South Africa, Canada, the United Kingdom, the United States and even France.

[16] Broadly, there are the Hindustani and the Carnatic strands.

[17] Rabindra Sangeet in Bangladesh is different. To a lesser extent, there is the influence of Dandiya too.

Ethnic Indian musicians[18] have also contributed to this fusion, as has Music Television (MTV), and international stars have appeared in Indian films.[19] This is no longer a passing John Coltrane, George Harrison, Miles Davis or John McLaughlin phenomenon. Much the same can be said of Indian classical dance.[20] Films spliced classical and folk dance traditions and combined then with Western dance forms, resulting in the mainstreaming of what has come to be called Bollywood dance. This is being choreographed, danced and taught everywhere in the world, and is also branded as a popular form of exercise. "Inspired by wildly popular Indian Bollywood movies, this exciting dance is packed with funky moves and stylish maneuvers, and guarantees a great full body workout. Get ready for an imaginative and artistic concoction of technique, energy, emotion and fabulous fun!" This quote is from a Singapore-based website.[21]

While the most famous fashion weeks may be those in Milan, Paris, London and New York, Mumbai has held a fashion week from 2001 and Delhi has hosted the Indian Fashion Week from 2000 and the Delhi Fashion Week from 2008. Indian fashion designers have been globally noticed. Perhaps there is a correlation with beauty contests. The Miss Universe contest started in 1952, but India did not win a title till 1994 (Sushmita Sen), followed by 2000 (Lara Dutta). The Miss World contest has existed since 1951 and India first won it in 1966 (Rita Faria), followed by 1994 (Aishwarya Rai), 1997 (Diana Hayden), 1999 (Yukta Mookhey) and 2000 (Priyanka Chopra). As with Venezuela, going beyond the product, this was a question of getting the packaging and strategy right.

By its very nature, cuisine cannot be homogeneous in a large country. And cuisine is also subject to cross-cultural and cross-country

---

[18] Freddy Mercury of Queen is an example.

[19] Such as Snoop Dogg in *Singh is King*.

[20] The eight classical dance forms are Bharatanatyam, Odissi, Kuchipudi, Manipuri, Mohiniaattam, Sattriya, Kathakali and Kathak. In addition, there has been the folk dance tradition.

[21] http://www.ymca.org.sg/Web/main.aspx?ID=a1054292-eec6-4cb7-b686-d62b 69aa7000.

influences. Had it not been for such influences, tomatoes, potatoes, chillies and squash would not have existed in Indian cuisine. Nor would there have been any presence of baking. And had it not been for the ingredients that go into Indian cuisine, Christopher Columbus would not have discovered America. Indian cuisine has influenced cooking styles in Indonesia, Vietnam, Thailand, Malaysia, Singapore and even the Arab world. There are estimates that there are more than 10,000 Indian restaurants in the United States, more than 1,200 Indian food products have been introduced in the United States since 2000 and the Indian food industry in Britain accounts for two-thirds of all eating out.[22] In England, Indian restaurants employ more people than iron and steel, coal and ship-building combined. The parentage of *chicken tikka masala* may be contested. However, the former British Labour Secretary, Robin Cook, described it as the British national dish, supplanting fish and chips. "Chicken Tikka Massala is now a true British national dish, not only because it is the most popular, but because it is a perfect illustration of the way Britain absorbs and adapts external influences. Chicken Tikka is an Indian dish. The Massala sauce was added to satisfy the desire of British people to have their meat served in gravy."[23]

The diaspora consists both of non-resident Indians (NRIs) and persons of Indian origin (PIOs). Excluding Pakistan, Bangladesh and Sri Lanka, the NRI and PIO population is estimated at 30 million, of whom, three million are in the United States, a little over one million in UK, almost one million in Canada and six million in the GCC (Gulf Cooperation Council) countries. There are 4,000 PIO faculty and 84,000 Indian-born students in United States universities. Though a neologism, the term Bollystan has been used for the region this diaspora inhabits and expressions like "diasporic diplomacy" have also been used, a sub-set of what has been called the practice of soft power. "Finally, there is a word for where I live: Bollystan.

---

[22] This amounts to 2.5 million British customers per week, http://en.wikipedia.org/wiki/Indian_cuisine.

[23] Speech delivered at the Social Market Foundation, London, 19 April 2001, http://www.guardian.co.uk/world/2001/apr/19/race.britishidentity.

For years, those of us with roots in India, Pakistan, Bangladesh and other subcontinental lands pondered what to call ourselves. The age of ethnic hyphenation produced "Indian-American." Then came the all-inclusive "South Asian" — inclusive, that is, of all but our adopted homelands. Today, we have *desi*, a Hindi and Urdu term meaning "people of my country." On the latest cover of *Another Generation*, a glossy British magazine for young, upwardly mobile South Asians, the hazel eyes of Miss World 1994 Aishwarya Rai gaze out from above the definition of Bollystan: "A state without borders defined by a shared culture and common values." Inside, contributors such as writer Pico Iyer and musician Nitin Sawhney discuss what it means to create in spaces that are neither here nor there. They dissect this process at a time when all things Bollystan are in vogue, from henna tattoos to Bollywood-inspired dancers gyrating on the big screen to rappers rhyming to *bhangra*, traditional Punjabi folk music that is often mixed with hip-hop."[24]

Within the diaspora, there has been a switch from the low-end, unskilled, semi-skilled and small-business category to the relatively prosperous professional and large-business category, a switch that plays a significant part in shaping perceptions. Before the Wall Street crisis, in the February 2008 Forbes list, there were ten Indians in the list of the world's top-100 wealthiest people — Lakshmi Narayan Mittal, Mukesh Ambani, Anil Ambani, Kushal Pal Singh, Shashi Ruia and Ravi Ruia, Azim Premji, Sunil Mittal, Kumar Mangalam Birla, Ramesh Chandra and Gautam Adani. Not much has been written about Indian philanthropy to academia abroad. Ratan Tata has gifted 50 million US$ dollars to Cornell University, Kiran Patel has donated 18.5 million US$ dollars to Florida State University, the Dhirubhai India Education Fund will be administered through the Stanford Graduate School of Business and so on. This is no less important in shaping opinion than Indian foreign direct investment abroad, estimated at US$17.43 billion in 2007–08.

There are also instances from sport and one does not always mean collective games like cricket, where the revenues are largely India-driven.

---

[24] S. Mitra Kalita (2004). Another Generation, *Foreign Policy*.

There are successes from lawn tennis,[25] chess,[26] shooting,[27] formula one racing,[28] badminton,[29] boxing,[30] golf,[31] billiards and snooker,[32] even if one does not mention the professional wrestler Khali. There is some positive correlation between performance in sports and levels of economic development. India may not have done that well in Olympic Games. However, the performance in regional or limited events like the Commonwealth Games or Asian Games has improved.

One can add to these examples of Indian soft power. For instance, almost 10 million Indian tourists travel abroad every year. There are almost 62,483 newspapers and periodicals in 101 languages and dialects. India sells 99 million newspapers a year, just after China's 107 million[33] and some of these are also read globally, on the internet.

"Hard power is necessary but has its limitations: Afghanistan and Vietnam have taught us that the side with the larger army does not always win. However, the side with the better story, the more attractive culture, and more numerous channels of communication, always does better than the one which only has guns. This is hardly news. When France lost the war of 1870 to Prussia, one of its most important steps to rebuild the nation's shattered morale and enhance its prestige was to create the Alliance Francaise to promote French language and literature throughout the world. French culture has remained a major selling-point for French diplomacy ever since. The United Kingdom has the British Council, the Swiss have Pro Helvetia, and Germany, Spain, Italy and Portugal have, respectively, institutes named for Goethe, Cervantes, Dante Alighieri and Gulbenkian. Today, China has started establishing 'Confucius Institutes' to

---

[25] Leander Paes, Mahesh Bhupathi and Sania Mirza.
[26] Vishwanathan Anand, Parimarjan Negi and Koneru Humpy.
[27] Abhinav Bindra, Rajyavardhan Singh Rathore, Manavjit Singh Sandhu, Gagan Narang and Ronjan Singh Sodhi.
[28] Narain Karthikeyan. F1 will begin in Delhi from 2010.
[29] Prakash Padukone, Puellala Gopichand and Saina Nehwal.
[30] Vijender Kumar.
[31] Jeev Milkha Singh and Jyoti Randhawa.
[32] Geet Sethi, Michael Ferreira and Pankaj Advani.
[33] http://www.wan-press.org/article17377.html.

promote Chinese culture internationally. However, soft power does not rely merely on governmental action — for the United States, Hollywood and MTV have done more to promote the idea of America as a desirable and admirable society than the Voice of America or the Fulbright scholarships. "Soft power," Nye says, "is created partly by governments and partly in spite of them." What does this mean for India? It means giving attention, encouragement and active support to the aspects and products of our society that the world would find attractive — not in order directly to persuade others to support India, but rather to enhance our country's intangible standing in their eyes."[34]

In their present form, India's reforms date to 1991, though some limited economic liberalisation started in the second half of the 1970s and acquired greater momentum in the second half of the 1980s. Consequent to liberalisation, has India's soft power visibly increased? The answer clearly is in the affirmative.

Though not a statistically robust sample, the number of times India has figured in cover stories of *Time* magazine is indicative.[35] Since 1926, India, in one form or another, has figured on the cover 31 times and 13 of these pre-dated independence. Of the 18 post-independence references, here is a flavour of what they had to say. (1) 27 October 1947, "The Trial of Kali" — "On a bed of stretched thongs in an open courtyard in Lahore, half naked, her head wrung steeply back, her legs rigid in a convulsion as of birth, a woman lay dead. Under the law of the English, whose writ ran for a third of mankind, it was fixed that whenever a person, however humble, died of violence or even unexpectedly, public inquiry was made into the causes of his death. If guilt seemed to fall upon another, a trial was held and punishment sought lest murder, undetected or held lightly, spread. In India and Pakistan since mid-August at least 100,000 have

---

[34] Shashi Tharoor, Making the most of India's soft power, *The Times of India*, 28 January 2007.

[35] The advantage of something like *Time* magazine is that the archives go back to 1926, http://www.time.com/time/searchresults?N=46&Ntk=NoBody&Nty=1&Ntx=mode%2Bmatchallpartial&Ntt=India.

died, not of germs or hunger or what the law calls "acts of God," but of brutal slaughter. Scarcely one died in fair combat or with the consolations of military morale...." (2) 17 October, 1949, "Anchor for Asia" — "When India's Prime Minister Jawaharlal Nehru needs to relax, he stands on his head. This is not the exotic mysticism of the fabulous East, but a practical way to drive off fatigue and make up for lack of sleep. Last week, as Nehru left New Delhi for Washington on one of the century's most important visits of state, his secretary discussed head-standing with the United States newsmen ...Nehru has a lot to learn about America, too... As a sentimental socialist, he has ticked off the United States as unrivaled in technology but predatory in its capitalism...A Farewell. Nehru's leave-taking from Bombay was such a scene as only an Eastern country in transition could stage. A harsh afternoon sun beat down on the airfield as the Prime Minister arrived, perspiring in his brown achkan (neck-high jacket) and white salwars (jodhpur-like pants). A small array of dignitaries, students and plain curious citizens waited near the runway...As he strode toward the plane's ramp after the review, the Prime Minister was halted by a shaggy sadhu (holy man), black-bearded and maned, who thrust a bouquet of chrysanthemums into his hand..." (3) 7th May 1951, "The Pandit's Mind" — "The legs-astride position of Prime Minister Nehru on the vast fence that runs through the world is of considerable importance to the United States. If this great, learned and widely beloved man swings a few inches either way — toward the democratic West or toward Communism — his shift can sway the suspended minds of millions in India and throughout Asia. The future of the democratic West depends in large measure on whether it can succeed in winning the confidence and friendship of the Asian peoples whom, until recently, it ruled. Western policymakers have hoped that Nehru — a man with known Western sympathies — is the Asian statesman who could lead a non-Communist Asia into the Western camp. Nehru has dashed these hopes. He has told his countrymen and all Asians that the West is their traditional enemy, and that the conflict between Communism and the West is not their concern." (4) 11 May 1953, "A Man on Foot" — "Trudging across this bleak land last week, surrounded by adoring crowds wherever he went, was a gentle, half-deaf little wisp of a man, dressed in the garb of poverty — a homespun dhoti and cheap brown canvas sneakers — but lighted by a flame of authority that has made him one of India's most notable spiritual leaders. His name is Vinoba Bhave (pronounced bah vay). He has no place in the government or any other secular organization; he is what Hindus call an acharya (preceptor)...It is not for his learning, however, that India's millions have given their hearts to Vinoba Bhave. They have done that because he, like their beloved Bapu (as they call Gandhi), has brought them a new hope. It is no new doctrine that Vinoba preaches. It only seems so, because the times have given it new urgency. Walking from one to another of India's 700,000 villages, he asks those who have land to share it with those who have none." (5) 30 July 1956, "The Uncertain Bellwether" — "Nothing has shaken Jawaharlal Nehru's profound conviction that it is up to him to set people straight on the facts of life. Incurable victim of what he himself recognizes as a compulsion to give advice, India's Prime Minister indefatigably ladles out instruction to family, friends, his 382 million countrymen and the world at large...Not long ago the United States. Supreme Court Justice William O. Douglas predicted that "the Big Six of the last half of the 20th century" would be Russia, China, Japan, Germany, the United States — and India. Whether or not Douglas' prophecy is borne out, India is already one of the world's pivotal powers, important less for demonstrated strength or wisdom or stability than as a bellwether, however uncertain of place and leadership, for the rest of Asia. In Asia today, there are 13 new nations, with a population of 635 million, which have won their independence during and since World War II. Against heavy odds they are desperately intent on gaining that other fundamental element of modern power — an up-to-date industrial economy. Obsessed by the desire to change from their primitive agricultural present, Asians are powerfully attracted by the example of the USSR (Union of Socialist Soviet Republics), which since 1917 has transformed itself from a nation of peasants into the world's second-greatest industrial power. The price the USSR paid — total suppression of human liberties and the sacrifice of two generations of Russians — does not appall many Asians as much as it does Westerners." (6) 14 December 1959,

"The Shade of the Big Banyan" — "India felt both angry and alone. The ruthlessness of Red China's behavior made a wreckage of some cherished convictions. There was no longer confidence that 1) Asian solidarity, created at the Bandung Conference, would outlaw the use of force, 2) Indian neutrality and nonalignment with "military blocs" would gradually lead the Communist and non-Communist worlds to mutual understanding, 3) the repeated pledges of "peaceful coexistence" by Peking meant that Red China was worthy of joining the UN (United Nations). The national disillusionment was so great that even Prime Minister Nehru took off his rose-colored glasses, looked hard at his giant neighbor to the north, and told the Indian Parliament: "I doubt if there is any country in the world that cares less for peace than China today." Threatened by a war it was not prepared for, India this week looked forward eagerly to the arrival of touring President Dwight Eisenhower. Indians appreciated the fact that of the eleven countries Ike is visiting, he will spend more time in India — four days — than in any of the others." (7) 12 January 1962, "The Natural Americans" — "John Kenneth Galbraith, 53, bestselling controversialist (The Affluent Society), Harvard economics professor and sometime speechwriter for Adlai Stevenson and Kennedy. Canadian-born Galbraith has had half a dozen Government jobs, since 1956 has compiled searching surveys of India's economy, and is now Ambassador to India." (8) 2 February 1962, "The Tea-Fed Tiger" — "From the Arabian Sea to the Bay of Bengal, from tropical Madras to the freezing Himalayas, election fever was rising last week in India. Government printing presses rolled around the clock turning out ballots for 210 million eligible voters (all citizens over 21). About 125 million of them — more than the populations of England, France, Canada and Australia — are expected to go to the polls this month in the biggest free election in the world...During the past 15 years, the United States has funneled $2.4 billion in aid into India. Though its interpretation of neutralism is often irritating to the West, India is the world's most populous (438 million) democracy, and could be a major force for freedom in Asia. Or it could merely be a confused and drifting giant, at the mercy of its fiercely aggressive Communist neighbor...Vengalil Krishnan Krishna Menon, Defense Minister in Prime Minister Jawaharlal Nehru's Cabinet, has always inspired bitter antagonism from opponents both in and out of India. Abusive, rude and overbearing, Menon, 64, is a Western-educated intellectual who despises the West, a passionate foe of old-time colonialism who consistently dismisses or ignores the new-style Communist imperialism. Nehru values Menon highly as a friend, confidant and traveling apostle." (9) 30 November 1962, "Never Again the Same" — "Red China behaved in so inscrutably Oriental a manner last week that even Asians were baffled. After a series of smashing victories in the border war with India. Chinese troops swept down from the towering Himalayas and were poised at the edge of the fertile plains of Assam, whose jute and tea plantations account for one-fourth of India's export trade. Then, with Assam lying defenseless before her conquering army. Red China suddenly called a halt to the fighting...Whatever the results of this peace bid tendered on a bayonet, India will never be the same again, nor will Nehru...In New Delhi illusions are dying fast. Gone is the belief that Chinese expansionism need not be taken seriously, that, in Nehru's words, China could not really want to wage a major war for "barren rock." Going too, is the conviction that the Soviet Union has either the authority or the will to restrain the Chinese Communists. Nehru's policy of nonalignment, which was intended to free India from any concern with the cold war between the West and Communism, was ending in disaster. Nearly shattered was the morally arrogant pose from which he had endlessly lectured the West on the need for peaceful coexistence with Communism." (10) 13 August 1965, "Pride & Reality" — "The ashes of Jawaharlal Nehru have long since disappeared into the silt of the Ganges, carrying with them the faint shadow of the rose he always wore in his lapel. Gone with the Pandit is the image of India as a moral bulwark of the "nonaligned" world, a pious mediator between the great powers. Gone with the jaunty jodhpurs and preachy pronouncements is the hope that India might soon be an economic success. Gone, too, are the pride and the confidence that inspired India in its formative years. India without Nehru stands dispirited and disillusioned, a land without elan where a rose in the lapel is somehow out of place. The death of Nehru last year was only one of the shocks that have forced the world's largest democracy to face reality. Before that came the Red Chinese attack in October 1962, which discredited India's foreign policy and exposed

Delhi as a military powder puff. Then last year the country was struck by its worst food crisis since independence, as riots erupted from Bangalore to Bombay. The shortages of grain called into question Nehru's economic policies, which stressed industry and paid little attention to the more basic problem of agriculture. And looming in the background was the seemingly insoluble deadlock with Pakistan, typified not only by the Kashmir question but also by the threat to India's borders in the desolate Rann of Kutch." (11) 17 September 1965, "Encirclement in Asia" — "...Yet another war smoldered in Asia as India and Pakistan wrestled for control of long-disputed Kashmir... Neither nation, fortunately, had enough petroleum, spare parts or ammunition for a protracted, all-out war. As one of the chief sources of weapons for both sides, the United States immediately decided to cut off their supplies. But there were still plenty of opportunities for troublemakers to fan the flames by pouring in arms — and a shrill chorus of support for Pakistan suggested that such accomplished chaos lovers as Red China and Indonesia might do just that." (12) 28 January 1966, "The Return of the Rosebud" — "Into the oak-paneled central hall of New Delhi's Parliament House — where Nehru himself had guided India's fate for 17 years — glided a hauntingly attractive woman, her black hair streaked with grey, her brown eyes moist and mellow. On her brown shawl she wore a rosebud, just as Nehru had always worn one as his talisman of grace and hope in a sometimes graceless and hopeless land...The patrician profile, the pale smile, the rosebud — all reminded the crowd of their beloved Panditji."

Two-thirds of the 18 post-independence references are for this period. After that, symptomatic of what much of the rest of the world thought, *Time* magazine lost interest in India. Democracy notwithstanding, this was a failed economic basket-case and deserved mention only in hyphenation with Pakistan.[36] (13) 6 December 1971,

---

[36] "India could not possibly feed two hundred million more people by 1980," and "I have yet to meet anyone familiar with the situation who thinks that India will be self-sufficient in food by 1971." These statements by Paul Ehrlich in *The Population Bomb* (1968) are symptomatic of those times.

"India and Pakistan: Poised for War" — "For months, border battles had broken out almost daily between troops of the two nations. The conflict that finally erupted last week along the 1,300-mile frontier was plainly big enough to raise the specter of a major conflagration on the subcontinent. The presence of Indian troops on Pakistan's soil escalated the dispute between the two nations to the point where full-scale war could erupt at any moment — a war that could also cause an uncomfortable confrontation of the major powers." (14) 20 December 1971, "Bangladesh: Out of War, a Nation is Born" — "Thus last week, amid a war that still raged on, the new nation of Bangladesh was born. So far only India and Bhutan have formally recognized it, but it ranks eighth among the world's 148 nations in terms of population (78 million), behind China, India, the Soviet Union, the United States, Indonesia, Japan and Brazil." (15) 12 November 1984, "Death in the Garden" — "The tragedy began on a bright, lovely autumn morning, with a light breeze blowing through the towering tamarind and margosa trees in the sprawling compound at 1 Safdarjang Road in New Delhi, the Prime Minister's official residence." (16) 17 December 1984, "India's Night of Death" — "The first sign that something was wrong came at 11 p.m. A worker at the Union Carbide pesticide plant on the outskirts of Bhopal (pop. 672,000), an industrial city 466 miles south of New Delhi, noticed that pressure was building up in a tank containing 45 tons of methyl isocyanate, a deadly chemical used to make pesticides. At 56 minutes past midnight, the substance began escaping into the air from a faulty valve. For almost an hour, the gas formed a vast, dense fog of death that drifted toward Bhopal." (17) 10 January 2005, "Tsunami" — India deserved mention only when there were tragedies and catastrophes. (18) 26 June 2006, "India Awakens" — "Even if you have never gone to India — never wrapped your food in a piping-hot naan or had your eyeballs singed by a Bollywood spectacular — there is a good chance you encounter some piece of it every day of your life. It might be the place you call (although you don't know it) if your luggage is lost on a connecting flight, or the guys to whom your company has outsourced its data processing. Every night, young radiologists in Bangalore read CT scans e-mailed to them by emergency-room doctors in the United States Few modern Americans are surprised to find that their dentist or lawyer is of Indian origin, or are shocked to hear how vital Indians have been to California's high-tech industry. In ways big and small, Indians are changing the world... That's possible because India — the second most populous nation in the world, and projected to be by 2015 the most populous — is itself being transformed. Writers like to attach catchy tags to nations, which is why you have read plenty about the rise of Asian tigers and the Chinese dragon. Now here comes the elephant. India's economy is growing more than 8% a year, and the country is modernizing so fast that old friends are bewildered by the changes that occurred between visits. The economic boom is taking place at a time when the United States and India are forging new ties." This was recognition of change and recognition of India's soft power, no longer restricted to cover stories, but featuring continually in other stories too. For instance, the word "India" figured 56 times in *Time* magazine between 1 January 1990 and 31 December 1990. Four of these were essays and four were related to business. However, between 1 January 2007 and 31 December 2007, the word "India" figured 109 times. Seven of these occurrences were linked to cover stories, 5 concerned business and nine concerned global business.

To state the obvious, the practice of soft power makes sense only in large countries, where there are economies of scale and scope in developing national identities. Has there been a co-relation between economic reforms and increase in India's soft power? There are two reasons why the answer is yes. First, directly, reforms have resulted in liberalization in external sector transactions, such as trade, foreign exchange and capital flows. Such liberalisation facilitates the practice of soft power. Second, indirectly, reforms have resulted in an increase in per capita incomes, even more pronounced in that segment of the Indian population that is globally integrated in various senses. Much more than in China, the practice of this public diplomacy in India is not state-controlled or state-driven. That's precisely the reason why it is credible and successful and that is also the reason why one does not need a policy to push it. There is no particular reason why these trends should not continue. "But the real promise for China and

India lies in the future. A country's soft power rests upon the attractiveness of its culture, the appeal of its domestic political and social values, and the style and substance of its foreign policies. In recent years, both China and India have adopted foreign policies that have increased their attractiveness to others. But neither country yet ranks high on the various indices of potential soft-power resources that are possessed by the United States, Europe and Japan. While culture provides some soft power, domestic policies and values set limits, as in China, where the Communist Party fears allowing too much intellectual freedom and resists outside influences. Both countries have a reputation for corruption in government. India benefits from democratic politics, but suffers from overly bureaucratized government. In foreign policy as well, both countries' reputations are burdened with the problems of long-standing disputes over Taiwan and Kashmir. Moreover, in the United States, the attraction of an authoritarian China is limited by the concern that it could become a future threat. The soft power of Asian countries, then, lags behind that of the United States, Europe and Japan, but it is likely to increase."[37]

---

[37] Joseph S. Nye, Soft Power Matters in Asia. *The Japan Times*, 5 December 2005. Also see, Mahizhnan, A. and Tan, T. H. (2008). New Asia: Projecting Soft Power, Institute of Policy Studies, Lee Kuan Yew School of Public Policy; and Jehangir P. (2003). The Rising "Soft Power" of India and China, *New Perspectives Quarterly*, Vol. 20, No. 1.

Chapter 8

Infrastructure Challenges in South Asia

Stephen Jones and Ramlatu Attah

This chapter reviews the key challenges for infrastructure policy in South Asia. It sets out a characterisation of the main features of infrastructure that make its provision by either the private or public sector problematic, as well as the routes by which infrastructure impacts on economic growth, and the main lessons from recent international experience. Available evidence suggests that South Asia trails many other parts of the developing world in important aspects of infrastructure access (notably in relation to the power sector), while plausible estimates suggest that investment in infrastructure in the region needs to increase approximately threefold to sustain recent economic growth rates. After a long period in which South Asia received only limited private investment in infrastructure, there has been a recent sharp increase which made India by far the largest recipient of investment commitments in infrastructure in 2006, with the transport and telecommunications sectors dominating. This followed a significant reform effort, but the rest of the region has made only limited progress towards increasing private investment, while the record in the key power and water sectors has remained disappointing reflecting continued policy constraints. The international financial crisis will make the task of raising international capital for infrastructure projects more difficult, but may create additional incentives for policy and financial sector reforms to encourage more domestic financing.

Introduction

The period since 2003 has seen a step change in South Asia's economic performance dominated by, but not restricted to, a doubling of the Gross Domestic Product (GDP) growth rate in India (Table 1), although the current international financial crisis is expected to imply

Table 1:   GDP growth rates in South Asia 2000–2008

Year	2000	2001	2002	2003	2004	2005	2006	2007	2008*	2009
									8.0	
South Asia	4.3	4.6	3.7	7.6	7.9	8.7	9.1	8.5	6.3	5.4
Bangladesh	5.9	5.3	4.4	5.3	6.3	6.0	6.6	6.5	7.0	
India	4.0	5.2	3.8	8.4	8.3	9.2	9.7	9.0	8.3	
Nepal	6.2	4.8	0.1	3.9	4.7	3.1	2.8	2.5	6.5	
Pakistan	4.3	2.0	3.2	4.8	7.4	7.7	6.9	6.4	6.0	
Sri Lanka	6.0	−1.5	4.0	5.9	5.4	6.2	7.7	6.8	2.8	

Source: WDI 2008 for 2000–07.
*Forecast based on data from Asian Development Outlook 2007. Figures in italics from World Bank (2008).

significant falls in growth at least in the short-term. This growth has put increasing strain on infrastructure sectors that had suffered from prolonged underinvestment and lack of maintenance, particularly affecting power and transport. Harris (2008) argues that:

> South Asia's impressive economic growth record…has occurred not because of the quality of its infrastructure but despite it. World Bank investment climate surveys routinely show that South Asian businesses perceive infrastructure, particularly power and transport, as a major constraint. A larger share of firms rely on generators in South Asia than in China and Southeast Asia. No South Asian city can supply water 24/7 to its residents. And businesses in South Asia hold larger stocks of inventory on average than do those in Brazil and China, a reflection of the poor state of the region's transport network.

The Indian Finance Minister stated in the 2005 Union Budget speech that "the most glaring deficit in India is the infrastructure deficit" (World Bank, 2006, p. 9).

The prospects for maintaining this growth performance, therefore, depend heavily on the extent to which improvements in infrastructure services can be made and critical bottlenecks overcome so as to maintain and improve international competitiveness. In addition, the South Asia region continues to account for over 40 per cent of the world's poor, with this poverty heavily geographically concentrated (particularly in rural areas and in the north-eastern parts of the region). The extent to which the benefits of growth are shared therefore also depends heavily on bringing about improvements in infrastructure, particularly through extending and improving access to transport, communications and power distribution networks so as to enable poor people both to access improved economic opportunities (greater integration with national and international markets) and to provide resources to exploit these opportunities.

Internationally, the 1990s saw a rapid increase in private involvement in infrastructure (Figure 1). There was a widespread expectation that the role of the public sector (and of the international financial institutions in the financing and management of infrastructure would progressively fall, and indeed the World Bank and other development agencies significantly reduced their role in the financing of infrastructure. However, after reaching a peak of commitments in 1997, private involvement in infrastructure (especially outside the telecommunications sector) fell away sharply, as the economic crises in Southeast Asia and elsewhere showed the exposure of private investors to significant risks, with a number of high profile contracts (particularly in the power and water sectors) requiring renegotiation or being scrapped. So the international context for infrastructure finance has been one of slowly recovering if selective confidence in the scope for private investment in infrastructure. The 2008 financial crisis has had

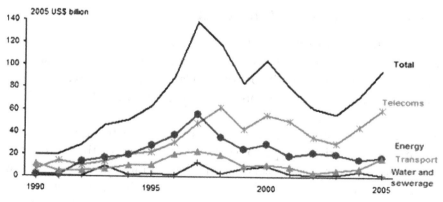

Figure 1: Investment commitments to infrastructure projects with private participation in developing countries by sector, 1990–2005

an immediate impact in sharply reducing the availability of internationally investible funds (the supply of available resources), as well as lowering expected economic growth (and hence infrastructure demand).

This chapter reviews the key challenges for infrastructure policy in South Asia. It takes as a starting point a review prepared three years ago (Jones, 2006) and seeks to update the information presented in that paper, review recent policy initiatives particularly in relation to encouraging private participation in infrastructure, and highlights key policy issues.

The chapter is structured as follows. Section 2 discusses the key features of infrastructure in relation to the problems for public policy that it presents, and summarises recent literature on infrastructure policy and the linkages between infrastructure, growth and poverty reduction. Section 3 outlines the dimensions of the infrastructure challenge for South Asia, in terms of estimates of the scale and type of investment required, and access and distributional issues. Section 4 reviews initiatives and policy responses to address these problems, focusing in particular on attempts to encourage the involvement of private investors in the provision and financing of infrastructure services. Section 5 discusses some possible implications of the current international financial crisis and issues for the future.

What is Special about Infrastructure?

Infrastructure poses special policy challenges because of its economic characteristics. These affect both the incentives for private provision of infrastructure services and the options available to policy makers. The key defining features of infrastructure include the following (Jones, 2006):

- The production of infrastructure services tends to be intensive in the use of particular types of capital. While typically there are technologies for producing services that have a range of infrastructure intensity (for example, different types of electricity generation technology) there are substantial economies of scale from using capital intensive forms of production.

- Most types of infrastructure investment have network characteristics so that the value of a specific investment is related to that of complementary investments that develop and complete a network. Hence there are both pervasive external effects and a non-linear relationship between output and the stock of investment capital.[1]
- Infrastructure investments are long-lasting and space specific, implying both high sunk costs (that is, once investments have been made it is hard to liquidate them and secure a return), the creation of localised monopolies, and the need for a long timeframe for the costs of investments to be recovered.

The main policy challenge for infrastructure (compared to investments in other relatively capital intensive forms of production such as most types of manufacturing) is that the substantial sunk costs involved means that investors in infrastructure assets face the risk of predatory interference. This may take the form of rent-seeking or a political response to social pressures to keep the price of basic services low. At the same time, the creation of localised monopolies that most infrastructure investment involves means that there is a need for regulation. The risks associated with the vulnerability to predation and the complex externalities involved mean that reliance on private provision of infrastructure is likely to lead to suboptimal levels of investment. However, public management of infrastructure investments is also likely to be subject to high levels of political interference and to risk inefficiency in the absence of effective competition and given the difficulties of regulating public utilities to provide appropriate incentives for efficiency.

Infrastructure also poses particular problems for financing. As noted in the World Bank (2006b, p. 11):

> Infrastructure projects are characterized by non-recourse or limited recourse financing, i.e. lenders can only be repaid from the revenues generated by the project. This limited recourse characteristic, and the scale and

---

[1] The returns to investment will generally be low for low levels of network coverage, increase to reach a maximum as coverage of the population by the network increases, and then fall as completed population coverage is approached.

complexity of an infrastructure project makes financing a tough challenge which is further compounded by two factors. First, a combination of high capital costs and low operating costs implies that initial financing costs are a very large proportion of the total costs. Second, infrastructure project financing calls for a complex and varied mix of financial and contractual arrangements among multiple parties.

The role of infrastructure for economic growth and poverty reduction is well documented in literature (see, for example, Estache and Fay, 2007; Agénor and Moreno-Dodson, 2006; Straub, 2006). The growth impact of infrastructure works largely through its impact on the costs of production for enterprises and hence on their marginal productivity. The poverty impact on the other hand can be seen as working directly through improved infrastructural services (for example, better health outcomes, reduced costs of transport and energy) and indirectly through the trickling down of growth via the employment linkage.

Recent research (Agénor and Moreno-Dodson, 2006) has highlighted several specific channels through which infrastructure affects growth. They note that most attention has been focused on the following channels of influence:

- Productivity effects: Infrastructure affects growth by increasing the productivity of other inputs such as labour thereby reducing the unit cost of production. Increasing productivity increases the rate of private return on investment and therefore the rate of economic growth.
- Complementarity effects: Infrastructure increases the private sector's propensity to invest. Growth in private sector investment enhances production capacity and therefore economic growth.
- Crowding out effects: Public infrastructure investment may also displace private investment thus having an adverse impact on long run marginal propensity to invest and therefore lowering economic growth. This channel creates an avenue for establishing a partnership between the public and private sector.

However, they also draw attention to other channels of influence including indirect effects on labour productivity, effects in reducing adjustment costs (for example, increasing the resale value of other investments), increasing the durability of private capital, impacts of health, nutrition and education, which may in their turn have a magnifying impact on labour productivity.

A recent paper by Estache and Fay (2007) reviews the current state of international knowledge and debate on major infrastructure policy issues, and draws attention to the considerable problems of information and lack of clear guidance from experience for policy makers:

- There is evidence that there is a general problem of insufficient stocks of infrastructure and, hence, of flows of infrastructure services, but there is a severe lack of information (particularly internationally comparable information and information at the household level on service access and costs) to allow the dimensions of this problem to be fully understood. There is also a general lack of information on public spending on infrastructure though India is an important exception to this.
- The relationship between infrastructure and growth varies substantially over time and between countries and contexts so that policy decisions based on generalised conclusions should be avoided.
- There are some reasonably robust approaches to calculating infrastructure needs based on anticipated demand but these approaches do not address the question of the optimal level of infrastructure provision.
- Although there has been much recent attention in the economic literature to issues of geographic location in infrastructure decisions this has yet to provide clear guidance to policy-makers. Estache and Fay (2007, p. 17) conclude that "we have little understanding of the dynamic impact of infrastructure investments on rural or urban economies or their integration.
- There is likely to be a continuing need for subsidies to provide affordable access to key infrastructure services for the poor, although in practice many regulatory and subsidy regimes have been poorly designed to serve the interests of the poor, though Estache and Fay (p. 19) note that "addressing the needs of the

poorest is not all that complex to do." The constraints to achieving this are likely to be political rather than technical.

- The lessons from attempts to privatise the provision of infrastructure during the 1990s are complex. Estache and Fay conclude (p. 25) conclude that "the privatization wave has delivered on some of its promises but not all of them." The focus has been increasingly on devising ways in which private sector risks are mitigated (for instance through upfront off-take agreements) and private investment has focused heavily on sectors and types of activity where risks are seen as limited or manageable, such as in mobile telephony.

- In relation to the critical issue of the role of the state, Estache and Fay (p. 31) conclude that "we know that governments will continue to play a key role as providers and financiers of the sector. We also know that governments have a regulatory role to play in a sector in which residual monopolies are likely to be strong. However we also know that the implementation of the mandate to deliver is plagued with potential sources of political interferences...Policymakers have very few clear yardsticks or rules of thumb they can use to set up reforms to get the public [sector] to deliver on any of its assignments — operation, financing or management."

Infrastructure Needs in South Asia

Infrastructure access in South Asia

Table 2 provides a summary of comparative indicators of infrastructure across developing regions. Specifically, it shows that there is a wide disparity and difference in the level of infrastructure facilities across Asia. There is also a marked disparity between East Asia and South Asia. This reflects different policy and investment priorities (Asian Development Bank (ADB) 2007) with the discrepancy in access to, and use of, electricity being especially marked. South Asia even lags behind Sub Saharan Africa both in the use of electric power and access to telephone services.

Table 3 provides a more detailed overview of current access to infrastructure in selected South Asian countries. For example

Table 2:   Comparative infrastructure indicators across developing regions

Region	East Asia/ Pacific	Europe/ Central Asia	Latin America/ Caribbean	Middle East/ North Africa	South Asia	Sub Saharan Africa
Access to electricity (% of population)	63	—	80	87	29	27
Electric power consumption (kwh per capita)	1,230	2,335	665	1,417	210	719
Improved water source (% of population with access)	75	90	94	88	76	65
Improved sanitation facilities (% of population with access)	60	83	89	81	53	37
Total telephone subscribers per 100 inhabitants	28	97	62	43	10	19

Source: World Bank Private Participation Infrastructure Database, 2008.

Table 3:   Comparative infrastructure indicators by country in South Asia

Country	Bangladesh	India	Nepal	Pakistan	Sri Lanka
Access to electricity (% of population)	20	43	15	—	62
Electric power consumption (kwh per capita)	100	380	64	—	297
Improved water source (% of population with access)	74	86	90	91	79
Improved sanitation facilities (% of population with access)	39	33	35	59	91
Total telephone subscribers per 100 inhabitants	7	13	3	12	22

Source: World Bank Private Participation Infrastructure Database, 2008.

Table 4:   Commercial perceptions of quality of infrastructure services

	Electricity	Water	Telephone	Road Services	Port Facilities
Bangladesh	2.0	3.8	1.8	3.9	2.2
India	2.7	4.6	5.6	3.3	3.0
Nepal	—	—	—	—	—
Pakistan	4.0	—	—	4.5	—
Sri Lanka	2.9	—	5.4	—	4.9

Source: Estache and Goicoechea, 2005 (1 = Worst 7 – Best).

Sri Lanka has near universal access to improved sanitation, compared to access for only 39 per cent of the Bangladeshi population. Among the South Asian the countries selected, Bangladesh stands out as particularly lagging in terms of the proportion of the population connected to key national infrastructure networks. However, these indicators hide huge regional (particularly in India) and rural–urban differences.

Table 4 provides some comparative evidence on the quality of infrastructure services as viewed by business. Business perception of infrastructure is worse in Bangladesh than in the other countries, particularly electricity and telephone scores. Generally, the quality of telephone services is rated quite high in most countries.

More than a third of Indian firms surveyed in the 2004 Investment Climate Assessment cite infrastructure as a major or severe obstacle to business expansion. In Bangladesh, this figure is 78 per cent. Power was seen as a critical impediment to business expansion and transportation came close second. In Bangladesh, firms experience power shortages 250 days in a year and, as a result, 40 per cent of firms in India, Pakistan and Bangladesh have their own generators. Businesses in Pakistan and India estimate they lose five to eight per cent in annual sales due to power related problems (ADB, 2007, p. 5).

Estimates of investment needs in South Asia

The rapid growth rate of South Asian economies has created a huge infrastructure deficit in which infrastructure needs far outstrip government resources. In South Asia, there are congested roads,

Table 5:   Estimated annual investment needs (per cent GDP), 2006–10

	Electricity Generation Capacity (%)	Telephone Mainlines and Mobiles (%)	Paved Roads (%)	Rail Routes (%)	Improved Water (%)	Improved Sanitation (%)	Total (%)
New Investment	1.8	0.7	2.0	0.1	0.3	0.4	5.4
Capital Replacement	0.7	0.4	0.5	0.1	0.3	0.3	2.2
Total	2.5	1.1	2.5	0.2	0.6	0.7	7.6

Source: Chatterton and Pureto (2005).

bridges that need repair, poorly maintained transit system and water facilities, all of which need repair and rehabilitation (ABD, 2007, p. 5).

Table 5 shows estimates of what is required to the meet the infrastructure needs in South Asia by sector given a GDP growth rate of 7.5 per cent.[2] These estimates suggest that such a growth rate would result in increased demand for infrastructure services that in turn would require investment amounting to about 5.4 per cent of the GDP. In addition, a further 2.2 per cent of the GDP would be required for capital replacement amounting to 7.6 per cent of the GDP in all. About two-thirds of these expenditure requirements are associated with the roads and energy sectors alone (Table 6).

The corresponding new annual investment requirement of US$62 billion (2004 prices) implies more than trebling of recent investment levels. In addition, a further US$25 billion would be needed for capital replacement of infrastructure, amounting to an

---

[2] These estimates are derived from an econometric analysis of the historic relationships between national income, population and demand for infrastructure (changes in the infrastructure stock), combined with forecasts of population and income growth. These estimates are, therefore, not based on what would be required to reach any particular target levels of infrastructure service provision, nor do they take account of the possible impacts of policy or regulatory changes on the efficiency of service provision, but rather they just project forward demand on the basis of past econometric relationships.

Table 6:   Investment needs by infrastructure sector, 2006–10

Sectors	Share in Total Investment (%)
Electricity	33.0
Roads	33.0
Rails	2.4
Mainlines	6.1
Mobiles	8.6
Water	7.6
Sanitation	9.2
Total all sectors	100.0

Source: Chatterton and Pureto (2005).

Table 7:   Expected annual expenditure needs, 2006–10

	Investment		Replacement		Total	
	US$ Billion	% GDP	US$ Billion	% GDP	US$ Billion	% GDP
SAR	62.6	5.43	25.5	2.22	88.1	7.64
India	49.5	5.52	20.0	2.18	69.5	7.70

Source: Chatterton and Pureto (2005).

overall expenditure requirement of US$88 billion per year. Comparing the estimated needs of US$88 billion with recent estimated levels of actual investment in infrastructure of around US$28 billion (although it is noted that there is no accurate data on the current level of investments), suggests an annual financing gap of about US$60 billion. India amounts to nearly US$70 billion per annum or 80 per cent of the region's total investment (see Table 7).

The International Financial Corporation (IFC) quotes more recent estimates from India's Planning Commission that suggest a similar investment requirement of US$320 billion over the next five years, nearly 30 per cent or US$100 billion of which is expected to come from the private sector, to increase infrastructure investment to the required level. The IFC notes that, although India has been relatively successful in increasing private participation in infrastructure that during the period between 2001 and 2005, private infrastructure investments have been less than one per cent of its GDP, as compared to two to three per cent of GDP in Brazil, Chile, and Malaysia.

These estimates of investment need are based on historic relationships between output and the infrastructure stock. Consideration of needs based on normative considerations (for instance, achieving the Millennium Development Goals, or on reducing discrepancies at the sub-national level) may imply a differing pattern and level of investments though comprehensive data on this is not available.

A key dimension of disparity in access to infrastructure is between rural and urban areas. For example, in 2004, 93 per cent of the urban population of South Asia had access to improved water sources, compared to only 75 per cent rural population having access. Disparities were greater in access to improved sanitation — 70 per cent in urban areas, compared to 34 per cent in rural areas (Sharan *et al.*, 2007). In India, the north east, central and eastern regions lag behind in terms of infrastructure indicators for example, electrical consumption, road density and tele-density.

The process of urbanisation is of particular significance for infrastructure policy. First, rapid urbanisation creates particular demands for new infrastructure services. Second, the pace and nature of urbanisation may itself be influenced by infrastructure investment decisions. As shown in Table 8, South Asia's rate of urbanisation has fallen substantially behind that of East Asia (dominated by China) over the last two decades. A critical question is the extent to which sustained

Table 8: Urbanisation (% of population)

Year	1990	2004	2006	2007
East Asia & Pacific	28.82	40.63	42.40	43.28
South Asia	24.92	28.29	28.85	29.17
Bangladesh	19.80	25.28	26.18	26.66
India	25.50	28.50	28.98	29.26
Nepal	8.90	15.32	16.28	16.76
Pakistan	30.60	34.56	35.32	35.74
Sri Lanka	17.20	15.22	15.10	15.10

Source: World Development Indicators, 2008.

rapid growth (as has occurred since 2003) leads to increasing urbanisation especially in India.[3]

Responses to the Challenge: Encouraging Private Participation

A major focus of attention (particularly from international financial institutions) in the effort to address the infrastructure gap discussed above has been the attempt to attract new private investment in infrastructure, particularly through public-private partnership (PPP) arrangements. Investment distribution of PPP has been unbalanced throughout the developing world. Between 1990 and 2000, Latin America took the largest share of private investment, with almost 50 per cent of total. East Asia followed with 27 per cent. Each of the other regions accounted for a negligible share. By 2001–2005, investment was more equally distributed. Latin America still accounted for the largest share of 31 per cent, Eastern Europe and Central Asia accounted for 27 per cent and South Asia 7.3 per cent. Since 2004, however, there has been a sharp increase in private investment commitments for infrastructure in South Asia, dominated by India (Figure 2).

Private participation in infrastructure in South Asia has therefore until recently been low especially compared to East Asia. Between 1990 and 2004, the region's 224 infrastructure projects with private participation attracted US$55.4 billion in investment commitments, far short of Latin America and East Asia (Bhatia and Gupta, 2006) which had commitments of around US$400 billion and US$200 billion respectively. India accounted for much of the activity in the region, with 76 per cent of projects. Over this period, the sector attracting the most private investment has been telecommunications driven by provision of mobile phone services. This was followed by energy and transport. However, private participation in water and sanitation is negligible (Table 9). Greenfield project accounted for more than two-thirds of the total attracted private sector investment. Divestiture came next in terms of the largest form of investment in the region.

---

[3] See Jack (2007) for a broader review of issues involved in urbanisation.

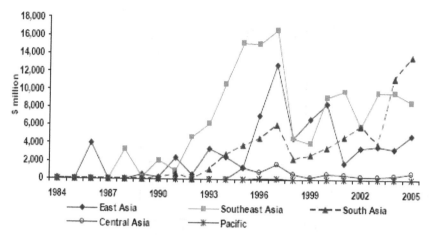

Figure 2: Private investment in Asian infrastructure, 1984–2005
Source: Sharan *et al.* (2007, p. 16).

However, the flow of investment under concession arrangement has been small. Management and lease contract accounted for a negligible part of this investment (Nataraj, 2007).

Harris (2008) reviews the characteristics of and reasons for this dramatic change, which made India, by far, the largest recipient of private investment in infrastructure of any developing economy in 2006 (with more than double the commitments of the second largest recipient, Brazil). Commitments in South Asia in 2006 were US$21 million. The increase was dominated by the telecommunications sector and transport, with the share of energy falling sharply compared to earlier periods (Table 10).

Telecommunications has proved particularly amenable to private investment throughout the world in the wake of major technological advances in mobile telephony. Sharan *et al.* (2007, p. 28) characterise the sector as:

> easily unbundled, metering and billing is technically easy, and the sunk cost is low…Pricing in the sector has been less politically sensitive than in other

Table 9:   Investment in infrastructure projects with private participation

	Telecommunications		Energy		Transport		Water and Sanitation	
	1995–99	2000–04	1995–99	2000–04	1995–99	2000–04	1995–99	2000–04
Bangladesh	438.1	651.3	554.9	501.5	—	—	—	—
India	7,456.8	14,321.9	7,165.6	7,559.8	1,272.8	1,854.3	—	223.2
Nepal	—	20.0	98.2	39.0	—	—	—	—
Pakistan	75.5	1,877.7	4,298.3	—	421.3	47.0	—	—
Sri Lanka	601.9	524.3	176.3	132.0	240.0	—	—	—
South Asia	8,604.5	17,612.5	12,293.3	8,232.3	1,934.1	1,901.3	—	223.2
East Asia and Pacific	29,304.5	17,612.5	43,589.9	19,697.0	24,636.4	11,293.5	8,987.9	2,852.7
PRC	5,970.0	23,042.7	16,916.2	5,359.1	10,802.8	5,201.1	719.8	2,332.8

Source: Infrastructure challenges in South Asia: The role of PPP, 2007.

Table 10: Sector share of investment commitments with private participation

	Energy (%)	Telecoms (%)	Transport (%)	Water and Sewerage (%)
South Asia				
1990–05	77	18	5	0
1996–2000	53	39	8	0
2001–06	17	64	18	0
Rest of developing world				
1990–05	33	39	22	6
1996–2000	33	45	16	7
2001–06	24	57	15	3

Source: Harris (2008).

sectors and technology has reduced costs, which has made the task easier. The development of regulation has advanced further than other infrastructure sectors.

The increase in 2006 was particularly related to the transport sector in India, where 40 projects reached financial closure during 2006. This has followed the successful implementation of reforms to encourage PPP in the national highway system, generally involving road toll contracts, combining a long-term concession for a stretch of highway with a requirement to expand capacity. There has also been success in developing concession arrangements for airports and some initial development of a private investment programme in the rail sector. The introduction of the private sector into water supply has continued to prove difficult, with proposals to introduce management contracts in part of Delhi facing consumer opposition.

The lack of progress with encouraging private investment in the power sector is a particular concern, given the evidence presented in the previous section above about how far South Asia lags behind other parts of the world in access to electricity and the use of electricity. Harris (2008) notes that:

> The region did see substantial investment in power generation in the 1990s, with a wave of investment in India and Pakistan and some notable procurements of independent power producers (IPPs) in Bangladesh.

But the power sector's continued financial weakness in most countries and the poor governance, including in procurement of IPPs, have stymied further investments. All countries in the region are making renewed efforts to ramp up private investment in generation.

In India, there have been a series of initiatives to address deep-seated problems in the power sector.[4] The sector has, for many years, suffered from a problem of unreliability in supply and cross-subsidies. This has led to a loss of the most lucrative industrial customers (who have undertaken their own investments in generating capacity) while State Electricity Boards (SEBs) have continued to subsidise domestic and agricultural consumers. Policy initiatives during the 1990s liberalised and encouraged private participation in electricity generation but did little to address the financial problems of the SEBs that had their roots in pricing policies. The 2001 Accelerated Power Development and Reform Programme aimed to promote distribution reforms and to provide transitional finance for SEBs undertaking reforms, on the basis of a grant of one rupee for every two rupees of cash losses reduced, and encouraged the formation of State Electricity Regulation Commissions (SERCs). The 2003 Electricity Act (embodied in the 2005 National Electricity Policy) sought to set out a comprehensive approach to consolidate reforms to generation, transmission, distribution and use of electricity as well as simplifying the process for undertaking investment in generation. While there has, therefore, been substantial progress in setting out an improved national level framework for power policy, much depends on its implementation at the state level, both in relation to pricing policies and ownership structures. By 2007, 24 states had set up SERCs, but only 13 SERCs had issued tariff orders, and nine states had unbundled or corporatised their SEBs (Singh, 2007).

In general, Harris characterises the region as facing an infrastructure policy deficit which is:

...manifested in distorted pricing, poor governance and accountability, and weak financial and operational performance. The policy deficit has had the

---

[4] This discussion draws on Bajaj and Sharma (2006), Ministry of Power (2008), Singh (2007).

biggest impact in the power and water sectors, where a lack of creditworthy off-takers has limited private investment.

Estimates by Devarajan and Harris (2007) suggest that pricing reforms to eliminate financial losses in the power and water sectors in India would provide a substantial proportion of the funds required for infrastructure investment.

The Indian Department for Economic Affairs and the Indian government has committed to raising infrastructure from 4.7 per cent of the GDP to 8 per cent of the GDP with a particular focus on transport, power, and urban infrastructure. Initiatives in support of PPP have included the Viability Gap Funding Scheme which aims to support the financial viability of infrastructure project thar are economically justifiable but not commercially viable (by subsidising up to 40 per cent of capital costs), and the establishment of the India Infrastructure Finance Company in 2006 as a wholly Government of India-owned Special Purpose Vehicle with the aim to catalyse infrastructure financing by providing long-term debt.

Other elements of the strategy to encourage PPP in India have included:

- Measures to foster efficiency and transparency in bidding, encouraging competition, promoting market driven tariffs;
- Standardisation of procurement procedures;
- Improving public sector capacity to implement and monitor PPPs;
- IFC is supporting an initiative is setting up an Infrastructure Advisory Services Facility with donor support to develop bankable PPPs in close partnership with government agencies at the central and state levels in response to concerns about the weakness of the public sector capacity to develop projects.[5]

A need for more rigorous and systematic oversight of the fiscal implications of PPP arrangements; a clearer policy governing the rationale for,

---

[5] See for example ADB (2006, p. 10).

and aims of, encouraging private participation; and more information and guidance materials have been identified as needed to encourage more effective use of PPPs in India (World Bank, 2006a).

Compared to India, PPP is much less advanced in other countries in the region. In Pakistan, there has been some initial experience with PPP in telecommunication, and power generation. There have been no PPPs as yet in water and sanitation. Sri Lanka has had some positive experience, notably with the Colombo port, Sri Lankan Airlines and a telecommunication project. In general, reforms in six areas are required to improve the environment for private participation (Bhatia and Gupta, 2006):

- Building a political consensus in favour of PPP;
- Moving towards cost recovery pricing to secure the financial viability of investments;
- Improving transparency — that is clarifying bidding criteria, competition in procurement, well defined selection process;
- Enhancing government capacity;
- Foster effective regulation; and
- Easing financial constraints through encouraging the development of long-term government and corporate bond markets, developing equity markets to increase the liquidity of shares in infrastructure enterprises, and regulatory changes to encourage the participation of banks and non-bank financial institutions (like pension funds and insurance companies) in infrastructure finance (World Bank, 2006b).

The International Financial Crisis and the Future

Implications of the international financial crisis

There are five main routes by which the international financial crisis which has intensified dramatically in recent months is likely to impact on infrastructure financing. The first effect is through an anticipated sharp fall in private flows of international capital as a result of the pressure on bank balance sheets and recession (or worse) in many capital exporting countries. This effect is estimated in the World Bank (2008):

> Even if the waves of panic that have inundated credit and equity markets across the world are soon brought under control, deleveraging in financial markets and an extended period of banking-sector consolidation is expected to cut sharply into capital flows into developing countries. Private flows into developing countries are projected to decline from US$1 trillion in 2007 to around US$530 billion in 2009 (or from 7.7 to 3.0 per cent of developing country GDP).

International financial institutions (including the World Bank) are envisaging a sharp increase in their lending in order to partly fill this gap. However, even the sharp increase in operations envisaged for the International Bank for Reconstruction and Reform Programme and International Development Associations would only provide an additional US$36 billion per annum.

The second effect is through increasing costs of borrowing as a result of increased perceptions of risk which will affect the ability of both governments and the South Asian financial and corporate sectors to raise funding:

> Developing-country interest rate spreads have sky-rocketed and equity prices have plummeted. Spreads on sovereign bonds have reached 650 basis points and those on commercial debt (which until recently had been the most important source of developing-country finance) have jumped to more than 900 basis points — up from levels below 200 basis points as recently as June 2008.

The third effect is through an induced economic slowdown (currently estimated to involve a reduction in South Asia's growth by up to two percentage points as shown in Table 1). This will reduce the demand for infrastructure though provided the effect is relatively shortlived this should have little effect on the viability of long-term investments. It will also reduce tax takes and the fiscal space for public financing of infrastructure investment.

A fourth possible effect is similar to that which occurred after 1997, when dramatic changes particularly in exchange rates and demand led to the breakdown of many PPP arrangements, contributing directly to the subsequent sharp falls in private investment in infrastructure in the developing world. In response to this, the IFC is developing an infrastructure crisis facility to provide crisis-related infrastructure financing in the short term:

> It could provide roll-over financing and help recapitalize existing, viable, privately-funded infrastructure projects facing financial distress. It could temporarily substitute for commercial financing for new infrastructure projects, if such funding is unavailable. The funding provided for existing projects would be for three- to six-year maturity, and the intention is that funding for new projects be refinanced commercially after a similar period. IFC expects over three years to invest a minimum of US$300 million and mobilize between US$1.5 billion and US$10 billion from other sources.

The fifth effect is the likely deterioration of the fiscal situation (caused by a mix of lower export prices and volumes affecting the tax base, and lower tax revenues resulting from the general economic slow down). This fifth effect could well impact on governments' abilities to provide matching finance for some infrastructure projects.

It is extremely difficult to make firm estimates of the relative significance of each of these effects for South Asia, including the extent to which India's recent success in expanding private participation (particularly in the highways sector) will be under threat, not least because predictions of the scale of the international economic impact of the financial crisis are being constantly revised. Assuming that South Asia's (and in particular India's) domestic financial institutions are relatively insulated from the direct effect of the crisis so that there will not be a domestic financial crisis, the reduced availability of international sources of financing may provide an incentive to accelerate reforms to deepen financial markets within the region, and to carry through pricing reforms (particularly in the power and water sectors) though these will continue to face political obstacles, so as to allow greater domestic financing of infrastructure. The sustainable means of financing long-term infrastructure will be to develop long-term financial instruments to be held by pension funds and other financial intermediaries.

Other Issues for the Future

The emphasis in the literature reviewed here has been on the scope and requirements for increasing private investment in infrastructure, although it is recognised that public financing will remain dominant in most sectors for the foreseeable future. However, public and private financing are best seen as complementary rather than representing alternative strategies. The conditions for effective public financing of viable projects are generally necessary, if not sufficient, ones for private financing. The key issues for the future are the following:

- The political economy of decision-making in the region has tended to date to favour the provision of subsidies to (selected groups) of current users of services, rather than encouraging cost recovery, or subsidies to promote access to the benefit of those currently excluded from service access. For electricity and water, in particular, the progress in improving access will depend on there being sufficient political commitment to move away from past policies that have severely hindered sector development and left large sections of the population unserved.
- Effective private or public infrastructure provision depends on progress in governance, in particular in developing transparent and independent regulation as well as in procurement practices. The scope for private investment depends critically on the development of public capacity.
- Likewise, there are important complementarities in the requirements for development of the financial sector to allow longer-term financing (to match the terms of revenue flows), and greater liquidity for bond and equity holders.

References

ADB (2006). *Facilitating Public–Private Partnership for Accelerated Infrastructure Development in India — Regional Workshops of Chief Secretaries on Public–Private Partnership*, Workshop Report, December.

ADB (2008). *Infrastructure Challenges in South Asia — The Role for Public–Private Partnerships*, Asian Development Bank Presentation to South Asia Finance Ministers, Madrid.

Agénor, P-R. and B. Moreno-Dodson (2006). 'Public Infrastructure and Growth: New Channels and Policy Implications', *Policy Research Working Paper 4064*, The World Bank.

Bajaj, H. and D. Sharma (2006). Power Sector Reforms in India, Paper presented at International Conference on Power Electronics, Drives and Energy Systems (PEDES).

Bhatia, B. and N. Gupta (2006). 'Lifting Constraints to Public–Private Partnerships in South Asia: The Way Towards Better Infrastructure Services', *Gridlines Note No. 6*, Public Private Infrastructure Advisory Facility.

Chatterton, I. and O.S. Puerto (2005). *Estimation of Infrastructure Investment Needs in the South Asia Region*, World Bank: Washington DC.

Devarajan, S. and C. Harris (2007). 'Does India Have an Infrastructure Deficit?', *The India Economy Review*, October.

Estache, A. and M. Fay (2007). 'Current Debates on Infrastructure Policy', *Policy Research Working Paper 4410*, The World Bank, November.

Estache, A. and A. Goicoechea (2005). 'A "Research" Database on Infrastructure Economic Performance', *Policy Research Working Paper 3642*, The World Bank, June.

Fukusaku, K. (2008). *Public Private Partnership in Infrastructure Development*, Japan-OECD–Vietnam Public Private Partnership Forum, Hanoi, March.

Harris, C. (2008). India Leads Developing Nations in Private Sector Investment, *Gridlines Note No. 30*, Public Private Infrastructure Advisory Facility, March.

Jack, M. (2006). *Urbanisation, Sustainable Growth and Poverty Reduction in Asia*, Paper presented at Asia 2015 Conference, London.

Jones, S. (2006). *Infrastructure Challenges in East and South Asia*, Paper presented at Asia 2015 Conference, London.

Ministry of Power (2008). Historical Background of Legislative Initiatives, Government of India, accessed via http://www.powermin.nic.in/JSP_SERVLETS/internal.jsp#.

Nataraj, G. (2007). 'Infrastructure Challenges in South Asia: The Role of Public–Private Partnerships', *ADB Institute Discussion Paper No. 80*, ADB Institute, September.

Sharan, D., B.N. Lohani, M. Kawai and R. Nag (2007). *ADB's Infrastructure Operations: Responding to Client Needs*, Asian Development Bank, March.

Singh, A. (2007). 'Policy Environment and Regulatory Reforms for Private and Foreign Investment in Developing Countries: A Case of the Indian Power Sector', *ADBI Discussion Paper No. 64*, Asian Development Bank Institute.

Straub, S. (2008). 'Infrastructure and Growth in Developing Countries: Recent Advances and Research Challenges', *Policy Research Working Paper 4460*, The World Bank, January.

World Bank (2006a). *India — Building Capacities for Public Private Partnerships*, Energy and Infrastructure Unit and Finance and Private Sector Development Unit, South Asia Region, The World Bank, June.

World Bank (2006b). *India — Financing Infrastructure: Addressing Constraints and Challenges*, Finance and Private Sector Development Unit, South Asia Region, The World Bank, June.

World Bank (2008). *Global Financial Crisis: Responding Today, Securing Tomorrow*, Background Paper prepared by the World Bank Group, G20 Summit on Financial Markets and the World Economy, Washington, DC, November 15, 2008.